BOOKS BY CURTIS W. CASEWIT

THE STOP SMOKING BOOK FOR TEENS

THE SAGA OF THE MOUNTAIN SOLDIERS

The Story of the 10th Mountain Division

CURTIS W. CASEWIT

Julian Messner
New York

5013

Published by Julian Messner, a Simon & Schuster
Division of Gulf & Western Corporation,
Simon & Schuster Building
1230 Avenue of the Americas,
New York, New York 10020.
JULIAN MESSNER and colophon are the trademarks of
Simon & Schuster, registered in the U.S. Patent
and Trademark Office.

Manufactured in the United States of America.
Design by Irving Perkins Associates

Library of Congress Cataloging in Publication Data

Casewit, Curtis W.
The saga of the mountain soldiers.
Bibliography: p.
Includes index.
Summary: Presents an account of the specialized
army unit of mountaineers from its training to its
role in defeating the Germans in Italy during
World War II.
1. World War, 1939–1945—Regimental histories—
United States—Mountain Division, 10th—Juvenile
literature. 2. United States. Army. Mountain
Division, 10th—History—Juvenile literature.
3. World War, 1939–1945—Campaigns—Italy—
Juvenile literature. 4. Italy—History—
Allied occupation, 1943–1947—Juvenile literature.
[1. World War, 1939–1945—Regimental histories—
United States—Mountain Division, 10th. 2. United
States. Army. Mountain Division, 10th—History.
3. World War, 1939–1945—Campaigns—Italy.
4. Mountain warfare] I. Title.
D769.3 10th .C38   940.54′0973   81–9662
ISBN O–671–41630–8   AACR2

A THANK YOU

It took many months and many kilometers of travel to research this book. One of my favorite trips was to a reunion of the Tenth Mountain Division in Italy. We climbed up a number of the old battlefields. I stood on Riva Ridge and Monte Belvedere myself. I talked to the ex-troopers all over the Apennines and we visited some of the hill towns together. Back home, it was exciting to hear the stories of other former members of the "Magnificent" Tenth Mountain Division. Most people were generous with their time. Some men supplied diaries, old newspapers, regimental combat histories, notes, maps, drawings, photos, letters, and other ammunition.

Dick Over, the signalman; Fred Nagel, the engineer; Bill Craine, the artillery gunner; Wilbur Vaughan, Plans and Operations; Bruce Berends, L. Co., 87th, all helped with valuable information. Feruccio Pilla, a former Italian partisan and now a lawyer, assisted with the project in the Vidiciatico region.

I'm deeply grateful to A.J. "Mac" McKenna, who arranged interviews and went beyond the call of duty to provide backup materials and pictures; to Major General J. H. Hay, who made corrections, and to Merrill Pollack, ex-*Blizzard* reporter, who pointed out some exciting episodes. I want to thank Chris Doscher (Montreal), John Campbell (Vancouver), and Hans Moser (Switzerland) for their hospitality. Karl Boehm, owner of the Peaceful Valley Ski Lodge, told me a lot about the Camp Hale atmosphere. Bill Dunaway, George Earle, Jack Smolenske, O. James Barr, Leon Wilmot, Fritz Benedict, George Ferris, Art Delaney, John Engle, Pete Seibert, Andrew Gordon, John Woodward, Earl Clark, Nick

Hock, Gerry Cunningham, Dick Wilson, Arthur Eldredge, Ed Richardson, and Gene Niblo lent a hand with this book. And Dr. Max Raabe helped bring me up to date.

I salute all these men and their families. Long live the Tenth Mountain Division!

Curtis Casewit
Denver, Colorado

Contents

Preface

This is a book about a special group of World War II daredevils who called themselves the Tenth Mountain Division.

Everything about the Tenth was unique. Most of these soldiers could scale the steepest rocks. They could soar through the deepest snow on skis. Many members of the Tenth had been famous ski racers. Others had been ski jumpers renowned for flying hundreds of feet through the sky. Celebrated alpinists, skilled hunting guides, and nature-wise foresters also joined this World War II army group.

While training in Colorado, the Tenth Mountain men had to cope with blizzards, subzero weather, and 80-pound packs on their backs. Roped up, they had to leap across glacier fissures. They had to cross and climb sheer ice walls. Later, the troopers learned to endure incredible heat, and fight with machetes and bowie knives, bayonets and mortars. Sometimes they'd have to wear white cloaks, pants, and gaiters for camouflage.

These troopers were also known for their high intelligence. Many Mountaineers came from good colleges. One general called them "smart and alert." To be sure, they were physically fit.

No obstacle seemed too formidable for these rock climbers and skiers who had been trained in mountain warfare. During the war, on a dark night after many patrols, the rock climbers of the Tenth scrambled silently up the difficult crags of Riva Ridge, a sheer 1,000-foot-high rock in Italy's Apennines Range. Icy surfaces and large loads of ammunition made the going slow. The slightest sound would give them away to the Germans on the rocky peak. The ascent took almost all night. But the Tenth Mountain Division reached the summit, surprising the enemy.

Twenty-eight hours later, they inched up another "impregnable," "impossible" mountain, Monte Belvedere. It took great courage to climb those long, barren approaches, to hurdle all those mines, and to buck the mountaintop defenses.

But everything went according to plan. The troopers

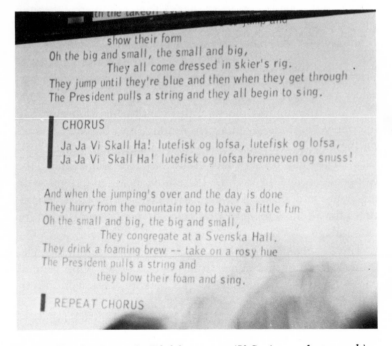

show their form
Oh the big and small, the small and big,
    They all come dressed in skier's rig.
They jump until they're blue and then when they get through
The President pulls a string and they all begin to sing.

CHORUS

Ja Ja Vi Skall Ha! lutefisk og lofsa, lutefisk og lofsa,
Ja Ja Vi Skall Ha! lutefisk og lofsa brenneven og snuss!

And when the jumping's over and the day is done
They hurry from the mountain top to have a little fun
Oh the small and big, the big and small,
    They congregate at a Svenska Hall.
They drink a foaming brew -- take on a rosy hue
The President pulls a string and
    they blow their foam and sing.

REPEAT CHORUS

The Tenth Mountain Division song. *(U.S. Army photograph)* scrambled upward meter by meter and eventually took this peak, too. "The Magnificent Tenth," as they were later called, also became the U.S. spearhead to cross the Italian River Po. And it was the Tenth Mountain Division which, in April 1945, liberated the Italian lake country from the Germans. Colonel David Fowler, who commanded one of the regiments, summed it up: "Your battle lasted just three months. But during those three months, the Tenth contributed more to the downfall of the Germans in Italy than any other division." A German general, after fighting troops in Russia and elsewhere in Europe, declared, "The Tenth was the best division I have faced on any front. They are elite mountain troops."

The Europeans have not forgotten the Tenth. Even now, almost four decades later, when these veterans visit in Italy, American flags are hoisted on red-tiled roofs. Welcome banners are strung between the pine trees, and the villagers turn out to greet the Mountaineers.

In the United States, the Mountain soldiers had a lasting effect on the ski business. Many big ski areas and resorts are managed by former Tenth Mountain people. Many ski equipment inventions were perfected by ex-Tenth members.

The Tenth's stateside training and overseas adventures make for a rousing tale. Here is the true story of the Tenth Mountain Division.

In the Beginning

By the end of 1940, things were bad in Europe. Hitler had invaded one country after another. Austria, Czechoslovakia, and Poland were in his hands. In April the German army had taken Denmark and Norway. A month later Belgium, Holland, and France fell. It was a time of turmoil. Even though America had not yet entered World War II, the shock waves crashed all the way across the ocean.

In the United States several outdoor groups showed concern about American military forces. The troops were geared for the flatlands and the jungles. What about the mountains? And how about surviving the winter? If the United States had to face Hitler's Alpine troops, would we know how to outmaneuver them? Our last winter warfare manual dated back to 1914. Would we have the right equipment to fight in the Rocky Mountains or in the Alps, if we needed to? Would we have the necessary antiparachute patrols in case of German invasion? Did America have enough men to cross the wintry wilderness in search of the foe? Would we have suitable clothing and weapons?

These questions nagged at many Ski Association members. America's skiers were fascinated by world events, especially by the expertise of Finnish ski troops. When Stalin's army had invaded Finland on November 30, 1939, the outnumbered, outgunned Finns were virtually invisible in snow. With especially light, narrow skis under their feet, they could dart from forests to harass the Russian invaders. Sliding at high speeds across a white terrain, the Finns would toss bottles of flaming gasoline into the Russian columns, then vanish. The Finns would reach frozen riverbeds on skis; then they would fire their rifles, put on skates, shoulder their skis, and skate away. The Russians were as clumsy as polar bears against such tactics, but they learned to employ winter warfare techniques themselves. By the winter of 1942, many Russian soldiers on skis also wore white for camouflage.

Some American skiers and sportsmen had spent their holidays in Switzerland. They were impressed by the white-clad Swiss mountain troops, the *Bergtruppen*. Other travelers had observed how their Italian counterparts, the *Bersaglieri* and *Alpini*, managed to move swiftly at high elevations, winter and summer. America had no such specialized troops, yet they would surely be needed.

Skiers wrote President Franklin D. Roosevelt in vain. Ski officials sent letters to Secretary of War Henry L. Stimson. He thanked them for their patriotic suggestions. High army brass were sought out by leaders of the National Ski Patrol, an organization that was formed during the late thirties in various American winter sports resorts. Consisting of volunteers, the National Ski Patrol quickly became known for assisting ski accident victims. Ski patrollers used toboggans to bring fracture cases to first-aid stations. In the higher mountains, volunteers learned to control and tame avalanches.

At that time about fifteen hundred men strong, the Ski Patrol was—and still is—of a semimilitary nature. Every patrol person had to dress in the same red parka. Although they were civilians, ski patrollers were always known for their army-type discipline, endurance, and nerve. To join the National Ski Patrol System, an individual had to be solid and speedy on skis. The patroller had to be familiar with rescue methods and master first aid like an army medic.

These mountain experts naturally worried about the war in Europe. What if America was attacked? They could train nonskiers in skiing, but the average new recruit would not learn to ski at once. "It will be easier to make soldiers out of skiers than skiers out of soldiers," said one Ski Patrol chief.

Meanwhile, all attempts to influence the military failed. The War Department still kept thinking in terms of the tropics. One day an NSPS delegation traveled again to Washington, D. C. Unfortunately, a heat wave was raging. In the War Department building, the thermometer hit 110°.

The Ski Patrol officials faced a sweating colonel. "What do you want to talk about?" he asked.

"Troop training in mountain and winter warfare, sir."

The Colonel mopped his brow. Suddenly he laughed. "Ski troops?"

NSPS leader Minot Dole wasn't discouraged by the many officers who in the next months passed him "along the line and out." One hot September morning in 1940 he finally worked himself up to General George C. Marshall. The U.S. Chief of Staff, the highest military figure in the land, listened quietly as the Ski Patrol chief started his long talk. It was so long that Dole wondered if he had won. He had.

In time, two War Department colonels picked up the ball. They turned up at meetings of the Ski Association. They accepted counsel from the American Alpine Club, which spoke for America's expedition climbers, men who had scaled the Himalayas, the Andes, and the Alps. The two army colonels could see that the Ski Patrol *would* be useful in case of a German invasion. If necessary, these Americans-on-skis would help defend the Rockies just as the Finns had defended their country. Patrolmen could become antisabotage fighters, trackers of spies, air spotters, guerrillas. They might parachute from planes, their skis following by parachute, too.

At last, the mighty U.S. Army was beginning to think of snow and started investigating the purchase of skis and boots, as well as other specialized equipment. By then, Nazi Germany had fourteen trained mountain divisions. Hitler and his Axis war partners—the Mussolini-led Italians—had swept into the Balkans. The craggy, rocky, up-and-down terrain of Yugoslavia and Greece was occupied. A need for winter preparations became even clearer with the headlines from Albania: TEN THOUSAND ITALIANS FROZEN TO DEATH. In June 1941 the German superforces attacked Russia, at first with spectacular results. They were to roll to within 11 miles of Moscow.

That winter, as the two giants battled in the bitter Russian snow, the U.S. Army took its first tentative winter step. On December 8, 1941, one day after the Japanese attack on Pearl Harbor, America activated a forerunner of the Tenth Mountain Division. This was the 87th Mountain Infantry Regiment. Formed at Fort Lewis, Washington, almost under the icy nose of 14,408-foot Mount Rainier, the 87th didn't enjoy immediate fame. A Dartmouth ski coach was the first to arrive. He almost turned around. Over the gate hung a sign reading: "Through These Portals Pass the Most Beautiful Mules in the World." The skier handed his War Department orders to the Military Police.

What was that? *Mountain infantry?* A major and several other officers seemed puzzled.

At last, the skier was told: "The 87th Mountain Infantry is *you!* You're the Mountain Troops!"

More volunteers soon arrived. Many of the skiers were

from Vermont, New Hampshire, Maine, and Massachusetts. While the 87th slowly grew to regiment strength, small scattered winter experiments went on elsewhere. In a remote Colorado valley, some of Admiral Richard Byrd's men—soon to be part of the 87th—were working with pack dogs and special sleds. Elsewhere in the state, a Ski Patrol leader tried to persuade the U.S. Air Force that it needed a ground rescue service. Stranded pilots had to be found by GIs who, in turn, had to be found by the Ski Patrol. When the air force was doubtful, the NSPS arranged for a test. A training plane would parachute a red streamer on any mountain within 50 miles. "We can guarantee that the Patrol will find it within five hours." A streamer was dropped on the Continental Divide and the location radioed to the searchers. They found the air force streamer in a few hours. Many of these patrolmen soon joined the 87th. At Lake Placid, New York, the NSPS was helping to train army skiers, and soon phases of winter warfare were being taught at Fort Dix, New Jersey; Camp McCoy, Wisconsin; and Fort Warren, Wyoming.

At Fort Lewis, meanwhile, the 87th was expanding. In addition to famous skiers and well-known expedition climbers, the 87th now also bristled with cavalrymen from New Mexico, artillery men from California, Montana prospectors, Idaho park rangers. The colonel in charge happened to be a flatlander who knew more about mules than about skiing. The army couldn't find a sufficient number of qualified ski instructors. It seemed that men who knew military tactics seldom could ski and the skiers who flocked to the new outfit couldn't teach military tactics. The only thing that was plentiful was snow. "So deep lay the snow that the three companies climbing 5,000 feet up Rainier had to tunnel their way into Paradise Lodge where three stories of the building were buried," wrote one of the troopers. It was soon more practical to move many of the Fort Lewis inhabitants into the Paradise

Lodge, a former ski resort. Skiing was at the doorstep there, and the troopers could train on Mount Rainier for seven hours a day.

By this time, there was no lack of volunteers. Recruiting had been entrusted to the Ski Patrol. Applications flowed in from all over the nation. Skiers couldn't imagine a better life than that shown on the posters, where Mountain Troopers, with snow swirling about their faces, braved the world in fleecy parkas. Magazines and newspapers carried stories about the military unit. Many civilians who had never tried skiing thought a trooper's life would be glamorous. After hearing about the 87th on the radio, a Florida tennis champion sent three wires to the New York Ski Patrol headquarters. In Richmond, New Jersey, one boy was classified unfit for military duty because of health reasons. Lured by the ski world, the boy volunteered eight times until he finally made it into the 87th.

Some volunteers signed up as a joke or for fun. Bored, adventurous radio operators, signalmen, and engineers asked for transfers from other units. Hundreds of civilians stormed the NSPS offices after learning about several Mountain troop celebrities. The star attraction was Torger Tokle, a Norwegian who was considered one of the world's best ski jumpers. Walter Prager, a Swiss skiing ace and famous coach, also aroused attention by joining. Hannes Schneider, then perhaps America's most famous skier, made news by sending his son Herbert and by sponsoring several other young men. A number of recruits came from the ski teams of Ivy League colleges. Many New England families vied with one another to dispatch their sons into the 87th and the newly formed 86th Regiment.

Of some fifteen thousand applicants, the NSPS eventually accepted eight thousand. Each candidate had to furnish three letters of recommendation. Ski Patrol officials, athletic

Soldiers in Alaska learned from the 10th Mountain Division.
(U.S. Army photograph)

coaches, sports club presidents, Boy Scout leaders, teachers, government officials, politicians—all signed such letters. Some young people sent affidavits from their priests and ministers. One candidate got into the unit after his choirmaster wrote: "Dick Over is the soul of integrity. I endorse him." Patrol Chief Dole's most unforgettable message arrived from Texas. The letter read: "My nominee will not become lost if there is no sun to go by; he will not starve if he has no rifle with which to shoot game; he will not freeze if he has no cover and snow is on the ground. I know, for I taught him myself." The letter was signed, "His older brother Hiram." Such credits were fine, for the Mountain Troops sought to attract outdoorsmen, including trappers, professional fishermen, loggers, woodsmen of all sorts, hiking guides, and forest rangers. Ranchers and farmers were generally needed to handle the burros.

With so many newcomers, the unit would soon be reaching division strength, and they would need a bigger post. After a long search, construction began on an army camp some 180 miles west of Denver, Colorado. In April 1942 workmen started an amazing job of leveling, grading, and building. Camp Hale's elevation (9,300 feet) was high; so was the price ($28 million) paid for the four hundred Camp Hale barracks. This was one of the most expensive army posts in existence, per square foot. By November, the days at Fort Lewis were over. The men of the 87th and 86th moved to Camp Hale.

The following July 15, the Tenth Mountain Division at last got its name. An army band was on hand. Suddenly, it started to rain. A real Rocky Mountain cloudburst broke loose. Lightning flashed. While the mountains turned dark, thunder racked the sky to emphasize the important occasion.

The Tenth was off to a good start!

CHAPTER

2

Action!

Because of the caliber of its weapons—76-millimeter howitzer artillery instead of the bigger 105s—the Tenth Mountain Infantry was designated a "light" division. The term light
also applied to the number of men. In July 1943 the Tenth's
strength—eighty-five hundred men—was slightly more than
half of a normal division's. The Tenth became known for its
animals. Special mule skinners handled about five thousand
burros and horses. Both would prove useful in hilly terrain.

By mid-1943, the division had been mixed up in all sorts
of strange activities. No American infantry outfit would ever
match the Tenth's "different doings." A detachment of men,
under Lieutenant Ed Link, flew to the Atlas Mountains in
North Africa. Throughout much of the war, they trained British climbers to cross river gorges by rope. Another detachment taught Polish paratroopers to ski in Italy. At about the
same time, a squad of Mountain Troopers went off to Hollywood to make ski movies. Other men spent several months in
British Columbia ice fields. There they developed and tested
various over-the-snow vehicles, including the "weasel" that

ran on tracks like a tank. For fun, the men had themselves pulled behind the weasels on skis. The sport occupied everyone so much that an angry officer cried out: "Is this the army, or a ski club?"

It was the army all right. Some of the division's units were shipped with their horses to California, and the skiers-turned-riders had to maneuver against a Filipino regiment.

Before the thunder clapped at Camp Hale, marking the Tenth's birth, other odd things went on. Lieutenant Frank Harper noted it this way: "The colonels and majors looked grave—the privates whispered—suddenly all skis and rucksacks had to be returned to company supply rooms." And in great secrecy the 87th was whisked away from Colorado. That June 1943, the three thousand men reappeared at Fort Ord, California. Here the skiers got the surprise of their lives. Uncle Sam's unpredictable army had turned the snow specialists over to the U.S. Marines.

The 87th learned how to handle bowie knives. The men received an issue of machetes and instructions in their use. Were Mountain Troopers being groomed for jungle warfare? It looked that way, although no one could believe it. A drill in amphibious landing and fighting techniques was next on the agenda. The troopers raced up and down boat nettings, jumped from landing craft, stormed the California beaches. They were to follow Winston Churchill's invasion dictum: "Surprise, violence, speed are the essence of all amphibious landings!" But *where?*

On July 27, 1943, the mystery deepened.

The 87th Mountain Infantry Regiment got off a train in San Francisco and onto a boat. They had a new commander, Colonel Roy Rickard, and a new, temporary destination: They were heading for the Aleutian Islands in the northern Pacific, west of Alaska. Action wouldn't be long now.

By mid-1943, the Japanese had elbowed their way onto

hundreds of Pacific islands. Convinced that they should rule the Asian world, the emperor's warriors had taken the Philippines, Guam, Wake Island, and others. Each piece of American ground had to be recovered from the invaders. This required tremendous U.S. manpower.

The 87th Regiment landed on Adak Island in the Aleutians as part of "Amphibious Technical Force Nine," which consisted of about thirty-five thousand troops, including fifty-six hundred Canadians. While tenting on Adak's beach, the soldiers learned what was in store for them. They were going to sail for the island of Kiska, which had to be wrested from the enemy. According to the latest intelligence, the Kiska garrison—half army, half navy—comprised about seventy-eight hundred Japanese.

The Allied counterforce was a considerable one. The First Special Service, for instance, had been trained in commando tactics and parachuting. The 87th troopers, after months of mountaineering workouts in Washington state and Colorado, were to scale Kiska's rocks. The Thirteenth Canadian Infantry had a reputation for able riflemen.

All through the summer, heavy and medium bombers dropped deadly loads on Kiska, a total of 1,310 tons. Warships blasted 600 tons of explosives into the island. Finally, on August 13, a huge convoy—nineteen destroyers, three battleships, five attack transports, fourteen LSTs, plus assorted minesweepers, heavy cruisers, and light cruisers—formed in the Aleutian sunset. Other battleships of the Pacific fleet had already sent off another formidable bombardment of Kiska. In addition, Liberator war planes were bombing almost every afternoon.

The armada encountered no opposition en route to their destination.

The Japanese navy held back, and no aircraft was sighted. On Kiska, targets hid behind a thick fog. As August 15 dawned, the ships' cannons blasted each landing site. The Special Forces slipped ashore first. Mysteriously, they drew no fire from the Japanese. Was it a trick? Ever since the sneak attack on Pearl Harbor, followed by many battles in the Pacific, Americans had learned to distrust the Japanese.

More troops pierced the fog that morning. Still no enemy activity. Like everyone else, the Mountain Troopers received huge breakfasts of steak and eggs. A few GIs were too excited at the prospect of their first combat to eat. Others wolfed down their food because they didn't know what the next days would bring. On these inhospitable islands, starvation was always a possibility.

Sergeant John Campbell, L Company, 87th, remembers that on his way to the beaches he felt "cool, detached, strong." Thinking back to that August 15, he says: "I figured that nobody could beat us." On the LST, Sergeant Campbell's squad shoved an extra pair of dry socks under their T-shirts, spare socks that proved useful after they had waded ashore.

The fog had grown so thick that they could hardly see one another. There was much speculation. Would some of Japan's three *mountain* divisions be on the island? By noon the Kiska beachhead was 4,500 feet long. Still no action. Officers who had grappled with the Japanese on the nearby island of Attu gave a sensible explanation. "The Japs must have withdrawn to higher ground," said one captain. "That's what they did on Attu."

The 87th's three battalions were among the first to land. They did so at three separate points, the objectives being cliffs and other elevations. Maps indicated enemy outposts and possible minefields, which could thus be avoided, at least in theory. Almost every hour, an explosion rocked Kiska. Mines went off. Most infantry regiments were not very enthusiastic about, or prepared for, the steep, rocky coast that the Mountain Troopers handled as though it were a sidewalk. Other Mountain men squished over wet moss and volcanic cinders.

The Kiska weather was miserable. In the afternoon a fierce wind rose, but the fog still held. This made reconnaissance difficult. Overhead, pilots grumbled about the black sky. From the air, the area was roofed with dark clouds. On land, radio contact didn't function because of the extreme humidity.

After each step, patrols would look and listen. Where was the enemy? When would they come? Veteran troops had warned the inexperienced 87th to expect sudden night attacks. Stories made the rounds about Americans skewered by swords, pierced by bayonets. On some assaults, the emperor's troops had been crazed with sake (rice wine). Their fighting ability—and their cruelty to American prisoners—had both become legend.

The yellow fog grew thicker. It drizzled. Now and then more mines exploded. The pincer movement to seize the island still continued. So far, no results. A corporal who led a patrol from the north shore to the south suddenly found himself face to face with another man. They inched forward through the fog. The other man advanced with a machine gun. The corporal had only an M-1 rifle, but he kept his hand on the trigger. Step by step they came over the moss.

"Bob!" a voice rang out.

"Paul!" shouted the corporal.

Recognition came to other Mountain Troopers. But as American units opposed one another in the impossible light, a few shots were fired.

Several wet days later, it was finally evident that Task Force Kiska had been hunting shadows.

The Japanese were gone. They had left the island around July 28, three weeks before the Allied landings. After deluding the "liberators" with antiaircraft fire, a small rear guard had been evacuated, probably by submarine. Military historians saw a silver lining, however. One U.S. Navy report about Kiska concluded: "While disappointing. . . the invasion was compensated by lives saved and lessons learned under conditions which were nearly those of combat. . . "

Unfortunately, the Mountain Troopers had to stay on Kiska for several more months. The island has perhaps eight to ten clear days a year, so the 87th soon came to hate the cold, damp, foggy climate. Men complained about the mud that "went to just below the hip pockets." For amusement, they challenged the worst cliffs. They caught fish with hand grenades. They played cards. Sometimes at night the wind was so strong that tents were almost swept away, despite their moorings to trees and jeeps. Early one morning someone forgot all about the tent ropes. An army driver got into a jeep and drove off, the tent flapping behind him The troopers' curses were loud enough to be heard in Tokyo.

That September the 87th also spent more time on patrols. They slogged through the cinders of Kiska's volcano. They poked through the empty outpost on the east side of the mountain. The troopers took a look at the rocky "Witchcraft Point," at "Hatchet Point," and "Hammer Point."

There was no enemy anywhere. That's how the song "*No Japs at All*" was born. Some of the words went like this:

> We learned how to ski and we learned how to climb,
> We learned how to stay out in any ol' clime.
> At last we were ready, our training was o'er
> We're going on record. We're going to war.
> The colonel he told us to get on the ball

Then gave us an island with no Japs at all.
We headed for Kiska with blood in our eye.
But G-2 had told us a hell of a lie!
Ten thousand Jap soldiers were due for a fall—
And when we got there, there were no Japs at all.

CHAPTER

3

Camp Hale, A Hell of a Camp

In November 1943 a portion of the Kiska veterans were transferred to other units in the Pacific, including the air force. The rest of the 87th returned to the country they had often dreamed about: cool, colorful Colorado; more specifically, Camp Hale. The camp had now been in existence for about a year. Some Mountain Troopers nicknamed it Camp Hell.

The altitude at first caused dizziness in some of the men. Unaccustomed to the thin air and put to sudden vigorous exercise, some Midwestern recruits actually fainted. New arrivals couldn't sleep and were slowed down during the day.

Smoke from the railroad and from barrack chimneys hung over the camp. The soldiers coughed all the time. (They called it the Pando Hack, because Hale's railroad stop was Pando, Colorado.) In summer, it rained every afternoon. The autumn mud was as terrible as it had beeen on Kiska. In winter, as the soldiers trudged up through the snows to 12,000-foot elevations, temperatures could fall to $-20°$. The dry air added to lung trouble. One night, to "create humidity," a new private flung pails of water on the barracks floors. The furnace went out and by morning everything was frozen. The Tenth Signal Corps men slept with 5-pound radio batteries against their bodies because otherwise their radios wouldn't work. Mountain Troopers slept on one blanket and covered themselves with another.

There were long periods when nobody got enough sleep. Days occasionally started at 4:30 A.M. There might be 15-mile marches through blizzards. Packs weighed 80 pounds or more, and the soldiers would be pulled backward. Without mercy, straps bit into shoulders. Welts developed. The army skis were often so stiff that they sank into the snow. Some Southerners and Midwesterners, recruited at the last minute, called skis their torture boards. Each time a novice lifted a leg, his muscles hurt. Each downhill turn was accompanied by pain, unless a man was a longtime skier. Climbing a steep slope proved hard on the arms as well. Until new skiers learned their lessons, they kept falling. They bruised, ached, caught the sniffles. Even experts had to get used to skiing with heavy packs on their backs.

Tenth Mountain "Basic Training" was made especially realistic.

For an infiltration course, men had to crawl under barbed wire for an hour. Then, suddenly, machine guns with live shells shot directly over their heads. Fifty-pound charges of dynamite blew up right and left. Mistakes might cause actual injuries.

Battle conditions were always made as believable as possible. New troopers were ordered to dig foxholes. Yet the Rocky Mountain ground was so hard that a pneumatic drill would have had trouble. Because foxholes meant survival, NCOs kept shouting: "Dig! Dig! Dig!" When the trainees could finally wiggle into their hiding places, a tank usually clattered up. Some draftees had never seen a tank. It not only

The mountain troopers in training.
(Archives of the 10th Mountain Division Association)

looked fearsome, but it rumbled right over their heads, spraying their helmets with dirt and pebbles. To the newcomers, these were frightening moments.

One day, during practice, a defective 60-mm mortar killed two young soldiers. A sergeant of the 605th Field Artillery, which was part of the Tenth, wrote his parents in Ohio: "These guys who glamorize war should have their heads examined." The sergeant also admitted: "I wish I could figure out a way of going without sleep. We do all our work at night. The wires are laid at night. On maneuvers we move at night. Then we're up again at 4:30 A.M." Some days, Camp Hale was one morass of mud, which froze after dusk.

Rock training was even more difficult than ski instruction. On the first days, novices were forced to balance on wet logs and to step onto huge boulders. Bound by ropes, they had to climb an almost perpendicular granite mountain several hundred feet high. If a man didn't look *down,* the climb was easier than the descent. To toughen the men, gloves were occasionally forbidden, even in cold temperatures. This meant scraped hands. At that point, a percentage of flatlanders often gave up. Another group refused to do the "rappel". In this frightening exercise, the roped climber descended a steep cliff at a 90-degree angle, paying out the rope as he went down, sometimes hundreds of feet. For men who had never been in the mountains before, Camp Hale must have held great terrors.

A "Tyrolean Traverse" was perhaps the most feared maneuver: it meant crossing high above a river gorge suspended from a rope. "If you even *think* for a split second, you won't do it. . ." one young soldier confided to his diary, "you have to shut off every thought."

Some fellows could do just that. Others had such athletic ability that mountaineering was no more difficult than a game of table tennis at the Camp Hale field house. Some of the troopers became such fine climbers that they eventually joined the two star instructors, Peter Gabriel and Walter Prager, in teaching new draftees. Many of America's mountaineering techniques were pioneered at this Colorado camp. The first new nylon ropes—and even a rubber rope—were tested here. Despite the great dangers, instructors themselves often walked the most narrow ledges without ropes.

The perils of climbing and the agonies of skiing disagreed with many soldiers who had been drafted into the division when more manpower was needed. Among them were former antiaircraft crews and nonvolunteers from Kansas, Nebraska, and Oklahoma. The men from Oklahoma suffered most of all because they were not used to the mountains. Heights scared them. Every day men washed out. Every day men claimed lame backs so that they wouldn't have to go on another 12-hour, 80-pound forced march. Requests for transfers streamed into G-1, in charge of manpower. Hundreds asked to leave "Camp Hell." They wanted to transfer— to the air force, to the marine corps, to the navy—anywhere *out* of the Tenth Mountain Division. Few of the original volunteers, the skiing instructors and ski patrolmen, ever

The mountain troops at Camp Hale.

wanted to flee. And Camp Hale kept an astonishing number of former professors and scholars. Among them was a former assistant to Albert Einstein, who spent his evenings poring over math problems.

Before the winter of 1943–44 blew its last blizzard, the weaklings had been weeded out. Those who hung on through the ordeals became toughened, and every day the Tenth's motto, "We conquer mountains and men," became truer. Men conquered themselves in this environment. Some troopers did it for the sake of those they admired in the Tenth. In their hearts, many of these young men wanted to be like Torger Tokle, the ace jumper from Norway; like Toni Matt, one of the world's fastest downhill skiers; like Steve Knowlton, the New England ski champion who later made the U.S. Olympic team; like Walter Prager, the Swiss super skier; or like many others.

Slowly, the Tenth Mountain Division acquired its reputation for toughness. The troopers became known as the roughest bunch in Colorado. Their training included boxing in the ring. On weekends when the Tenth sallied forth to ski for pleasure—they had their own lift-served terrain on nearby Cooper Hill—the fellows were known for their murderous speeds. Having been ski racers, many of them now streaked straight down.

These speeds caused collisions with civilian skiers. Men were flung into the trees. Legs were broken. Bloody noses were frequent. On January 7, 1944, Hale's Headquarters Bulletin warned: "MP [Military Police] will now be posted on Cooper Hill, to enforce the rules. Uncontrolled skiing will not be tolerated. Anyone found skiing without control will be kicked off the hill." In nearby towns, the Tenth's MPs became famous for hitting first and asking questions later. And the Mountaineers themselves tore their attackers apart. Woe to those who tried starting a brawl with a Camp Hale man!

Camp Hale during World War II. The area is now a campground.
(U.S. Army photograph)

The U.S. Air Force fly-boys avoided entanglements with the
skiers. When they met in bars or on the streets of the Colorado towns, airmen would quietly shove off at the sight of the
Mountain Troopers. "We felt like supermen," recalls one sergeant. With their heavy square boots, the man of the Tenth
even looked different. They didn't plan to lose a fight. Ob-
viously, Hitler and Hirohito (whose pictures hung in all mess
halls) would have to reckon with a rugged group.

World War II held great meaning for these soldiers. Quite
a few of them had their own reasons to hate Nazi Germany.

As well-traveled Americans, they had visited Hitler's country before the war. These men knew what the dictator was up to. They knew that he loathed blacks, persecuted Jews, and mistreated other minorities. A few Mountain Troopers, before becoming naturalized American citizens, had been driven out of their German homes because of religion or race. Norwegians had fled when the Nazis occupied their country. The Tenth Mountain Division was a home to Austrian refugees.

These foreign troopers sometimes aroused suspicion in nearby Leadville. The cry "Someone is speaking German!"

Training at Camp Hale.
(Archives of the 10th Mountain Division Association)

often went up in the old Colorado mining community. Camp Hale's Intelligence officers had to rush to the rescue and explain that these were not German spies. None of these men was an escaped German prisoner of war.

Some of the Mountain Troopers had strange quirks. Several sergeants of Finnish extraction, for instance, liked to take off all their clothes and roll in the snow just outside the camp. To invent faster ski waxes, men enjoyed smelling up the barracks by melting down old phonograph records or candy bars. These activities would not have been possible in any other division. No officer made a fuss when someone from the 87th bought a goat at a Denver auction, even though the pet galloped through camp Hale, creating havoc.

Nor did the brass worry too much about a whole squad turning Leadville's Vendome Hotel into a nighttime mountaineering area. Men fixed ropes to hotel fire escapes and let themselves down before dawn. Guests awoke. Windows broke. The guilty ones were already on a high-altitude march before anyone could follow.

Great feats of stamina seemed commonplace. On a bet, two soldiers used their furlough to walk from Pando to Glenwood Springs, 75 miles away. They completed the mountain hike in 21 hours without a minute's sleep. They had one candy bar each for food. On another occasion, a field artillery regiment hiked from Colorado Springs to Camp Hale, some 170 miles. One soldier wrote his parents: "Medics had to take care of five hundred blisters."

All these events welded the Tenth into a unique unit. Many of the men had known each other before joining. Many were lifelong friends. The *esprit de corps*, made up of pride and comradeship, could not be matched by many other divisions. To visitors, the parading Tenth must have looked most impressive. The white uniforms, the white parkas, the white skis; the tanned, cocky faces; the young voices singing that they were "Best by far/We'll win this goddamned war"—all this must have had an impact.

Day-to-day life bristled with adventure. What other division tested snow vehicles and rescue toboggans or learned to snowshoe? Who but the Tenth troopers were introduced to avalanche dangers and avalanche rescues? A famous Arctic explorer taught them how to build igloos and other snow caves, and many nights the men actually slept in these snow houses. Birger Toreson, a Tenth member who had lived in the Arctic, showed the troopers how they could keep their hands from freezing. He greased their palms with raw bacon strips before long marches. The Tenth Mountain Division

Training on bivouac near Camp Hale. *(A.J. McKenna)*

also learned the use of steel spikes under their boots. These "crampons" gripped ice walls on nearby ice cliffs.

Meanwhile, Tenth Mountain artillery shot down snow overhangs, called cornices. (If a soldier were to ski under such a cornice, it might crush him.) When a snow slope was too dangerous, the troopers sometimes tossed hand grenades. The explosion caused the snow masses to cascade downhill without injuring anyone.

The men moved at such high altitudes that they could converse on their radios with bomber pilots. One afternoon, just before landing at a Colorado airfield, a pilot reported to the ground crews: "I'm at eight thousand feet and gliding, gliding!" Immediately, a strange voice crackled: "And I am at twelve thousand feet and walking, walking!" It was a Mountain Trooper high above Camp Hale.

Peaks rose on all sides from the camp, and the troopers explored Sheep Mountain and Wearyman Peak and Jacques Peak. They sometimes fought these mountains to the limits of their endurance.

One test began on Sunday, March 26, 1944, as part of a war exercise that went under the name of "D" Series. At dawn that day, about twelve thousand of Camp Hale's fifteen thousand men filed up the steeply rising Tennessee Pass. On this occasion they didn't turn toward Homestake Peak, where they trained most of the time. Instead, they headed for Ptarmigan Peak. It was −10° when the sun rose. The first men up had the hardest task. They had to break trail with their skis.

At first the troopers felt fine. They were in the best physical condition. Long distance cross-country ski races had honed their bodies. Arduous rock climbs had slimmed them. The men could look up to the tough, lean officers and to the famous skiers who led them.

The companies strung out single file. The heights were reached by means of zigzagging, and the men on top could see the long white snake that followed. The rhythm was well established by the leaders, and the skis had good upward traction because the men glued sealskins under the surface. The fur prevented them from slipping backward.

As usual, packs were heavily loaded: sleeping bags alone weighed 20 pounds. The men carried shovels, 10-pound rifles, pots and pans, ammunition. They lugged extra clothes in case of blizzards. The food followed on tanklike weasels that had been painted as white as the snow, inside as well as outside. Mortars were put on toboggans that were drawn by skiers. Some of the artillery was packed on mules. A mule named Hitler was used by a company dentist to carry his instruments and drills, which worked by means of foot pedals. "Hitler" also brought a dismantled dental chair that could be put together again for use in the field. The caravan included other mules, each loaded with 200 pounds of engineering ma-

Training in mortars at Camp Hale. *(A.J. McKenna)*

terial. Several genuine Arctic sleds, each pulled by a team of nine dogs, sped ahead.

Chaplains on skis took part in "D" Series. Surgeons and medics accompanied the troops. And plenty of support units —the 110th Signal Company, the 126th Engineers, the 605th Field Artillery Battalion—also came along.

The second morning out, as the Rockies grew higher, temperatures fell. It was suddenly −20°. Although shielded against this cold by parkas and heavy clothes, the men had difficulty breathing. Their lungs stung. A few soldiers wore chamois masks, which protected their skin against possible frostbite. The next day, temperatures sank to −30°. A slight wind whipped into their faces. Hoods and caps covered their ears. It grew so cold that a corporal, who took out his eyeglasses to check a map, had his frames fall apart in his hands. The plastic had become brittle from the cold. To get a better grip on a spare can of gasoline, one weasel driver took off his mittens. The can immediately stuck to his bare skin. The metal had to be pried loose by a buddy.

During the next days, as the war games went on, rifles wouldn't fire. Communications bogged down because radio batteries froze even when the men kept them under their sweaters. Walkie-talkies, mounted on ski poles, failed to operate.

Some GIs fell ill with pneumonia and had to be brought out of the wilderness on toboggans. While the medics were busy, several units took "prisoners." Planted explosives gave a real battle feeling. "Hit the ground!" yelled the sergeants. To make the "D" Series seem genuine, no fires were allowed because they would attract "the enemy." Blackout ruled at night. Before turning in, men brushed the snow off their parkas with special little brooms. This prevented the flakes from melting and then freezing on the sleeping soldiers.

A week out of camp, the troops ran into a blizzard. Soon the snow was so deep that some of the special vehicles got stuck. Food supplies dwindled. Instead of turning back, all but the sick continued, by orders of Major General Lloyd Jones, commanding officer. It was to be the worst "D" Series they had ever experienced, but the officers—Brigadier General David Ruffner and Colonel Robinson Duff—stuck it out with the men.

After several more days, the sky cleared. The snow became so bright that the men had to put on sunglasses to protect their eyes from snow blindness.

At last the men reached the base of Ptarmigan Peak. This meant another hardy zigzag climb. Everyone itched with sweat. Fatigue began to mark even the toughest faces. The tempo slowed down.

On Easter Sunday 1944 the weather warmed up a bit. Then, by a quirk of nature, a wet, heavy snow began. It melted on the men; their clothing was soaked with water. When the mercury dropped, the men's clothing turned to ice.

The new snow (eight more feet) was so deep that supply vehicles could not reach the snowbound Mountain Troopers high in the back country. Thus, for three days, there was hardly anything to eat. Even former ski racers had trouble coping with empty stomachs.

The "D" Series lasted almost a month. An official report concluded: "This maneuver . . . was perhaps the most grueling training test ever given to any U.S. Army division. It was performed under the most adverse and difficult conditions. . . ."

When the troopers finally got back to Camp Hale, army doctors counted one hundred cases of frostbite. The Hale hospital had almost two dozen filled beds. All the nearby civilian hospitals were booked with skiers suffering from exposure, pneumonia, and fever. Had the army been too rough on the Tenth Mountain Division?

Someday the troopers would be grateful for that Colorado month. One corporal summed it up in his diary: "Anyone who survives these last weeks will survive anything."

4

Ordeals at a New Camp

Early one June morning in 1944 a sergeant of the 110th Mountain Signal Company tensed as he bent over his desk. He was alone in this room of the Message Center, which tied Camp Hale to the War Department in Washington, D.C. The sergeant had special "secret clearance" to work in this Colorado center. Only a few particular Mountain Troopers were allowed in this room. It was Camp Hale's nerve center. Every order had to pass through here in code.

The decoding operation required extensive training, for the secret messages arrived both in figures and in letters. The code for "Pando, Colorado," for example, could be "CUGC" or "0881." Messages could come in a combination of numbers and letters. All codes were occasionally changed, so that enemy spies could not decipher them. Whatever happened, the entire division, including G-1 (Personnel), G-2 (Intelligence), G-3 (Training), and G-4 (Supplies), depended on the accuracy of the signalman. This particular sergeant had become so accurate that some messages were now routine to him. But that morning he had to look twice at a top secret order just in from the General Staff: "Prepare division for transfer to Camp Swift."

The NCO took the decoded message to his officer, who gave it to General Jones. None of the three men could reveal their knowledge until the troops stood on the regimental parade grounds. Only then did each regiment's commander announce that they were to leave Camp Hale. All skis and winter equipment would be left behind.

No one knew anything about Camp Swift. It turned out that it was in Texas, about 40 miles from Austin.

After the cool Colorado summer, the sweaty journey to Texas was an unpleasant one. First the troops went through the warm plains of Kansas, then south to Oklahoma. Then still farther south into the heat of Texas. At the end of June, the sweating Mountain Troopers finally rolled into Camp Swift. The Austin Weather Bureau gave the local temperature as 102° in the shade.

That summer, Texas was hot, hot, hot.

At first the troopers had only their winter uniforms. The thick cloth stuck to their skin. Feet itched in thick socks. Perspiration poured down the men's spines as they kept asking themselves, why Camp Swift? To the average soldier, this question remained unanswered until World War II was over. It seems that no one wanted the Tenth Mountain Division in mid-1944. A military historian learned eventually that Chief of Staff George C. Marshall had offered the Mountain Troopers to several corps commanders. All of them turned down the unit. It was true that supply problems were difficult enough for the average division. Ski troops required special gear, and the commanders must have wondered where they would get equipment like toboggans and dogsleds when deploying these troops. "So the Tenth was thrown into west Texas," wrote one of the unit's analysts. "Perhaps the high military thinkers had decided to scrap over two years of mountain training to produce a standardized division out of the overtrained Tenth."

The troopers quickly agreed that the new army post had a few consoling features. Camp Swift was prettier than Camp Hale, even if the men missed the encircling mountains. Camp Swift provided several big swimming pools. A small river ran through green meadows with trees. There was no smoke and there would be no winter heating problems. Camp Swift had a church, several clubs, and lots of motion pictures and sports facilities of all kinds. There was a symphony orchestra. After a while, there would be passes to Austin, which was much bigger than Leadville, Colorado. There would be girls in Austin and more amusements.

But not far from Camp Swift the sandy, dusty, flat plains began. The Mountain Troopers were allowed a week to get accustomed to the broiling heat and to the mountainless landscape. Then on July 15, while the thermometer rose and rose, the Tenth Mountain Division gathered for a parade. "Today is your first anniversary," the general told them. About one thousand civilians from Austin arrived to look at the perspiring, unhappy regiments. Camp Swift's parade ground had been hosed down with water. But it was still 103° in the shade. The troopers' heads steamed under the steel helmets. Buttoned collars and ties were a torture.

After a few days the workouts started again. The Tenth had to be "whipped into combat shape," as one officer put it. This meant hours of foxhole digging and running in the broiling sun, days of rifle drills, weeks on the shooting range, bayonet training, and calisthenics, and more parades and endless marches through the dusty flatness. It was one thing to slide on skis even for 150 miles, up and down the cool valleys, but quite another to cross the desert, which the troopers hated.

Despite the army censors, who judged all mail, an artillery sergeant managed to send a letter to Ohio. Sergeant Bill

Crain's message was clear enough. "Dear Mother and Dad," he wrote. "Can you imagine these people? First trying to freeze us all winter? And now trying to bake us to a crisp? The sweat is running off me. The mules are slowly withering away in the heat. I feel sorry for them standing out in that sun." The artillery sergeant had counted the days he had been at Camp Swift—fifty-one. Of these, thirty-two had been spent in the desert on maneuvers.

Here every unit had its work cut out. Engineers built pontoon bridges, which would someday be needed to cross battle zone rivers. The engineers tested special hoists for the wounded. Signalmen strung wires and looked after communications. The infantry played war, as always. Regiments were broken down into the smallest units, such as platoons and squads, and received instruction in the proper use of firepower—with live ammunition. The platoons and squads sharpened their skills in hitting a foe swiftly and independently. Someday, all this knowledge would come in handy. But during the tortuous maneuvers, many of the troopers longed for winter warfare.

In addition to the hard workouts, the troops faced lizards, flies, poison ivy, and poison oak. An NCO caught two deadly black widow spiders. To those from Colorado, everything seemed new and strange and dangerous. A man was bitten by a rattlesnake in a nearby swamp. The troopers complained about Camp Swift's showers ("just a pail with holes"), and they griped about the camp food ("chicken, chicken, chicken"). Troopers beefed about their daily duties, such as KP (Kitchen Police), which meant cleaning garbage cans and grease traps.

The Tenth's shoulder patch—crossed bayonets with the word "Mountain" over them—had no meaning now. Morale was sinking. Camp Swift's military super discipline was partly responsible. Army rules now extended to the "speed marches" in the plains. One division order stated:

> March discipline must be rigorously enforced in every aspect. If a man is forced to stop to repair or readjust equipment or because of illness or an injury, he should immediately fall out of the column, and should not try to regain his place until the next halt. All commanders must give continuous attention to keeping marching formations closed to proper distances especially when weather conditions deteriorate rapidly. Ordinarily this can only be accomplished at halts. Straggling must not be tolerated and the taking of shortcuts should be forbidden.

Most troopers would always remember one particular 25-mile speed march. The men were racked by thirst almost from the start. Several fainted from heat exhaustion. Nevertheless, a colonel insisted on regulations. His name was Colonel R.E. Duff, and they called him the "Terror of Camp Swift." The officer would suddenly ride up in his jeep, stop the troopers, and inspect them, despite the heat and the casualties. On that particular march, he reprimanded several Mountaineers for having rolled up their fatigue sleeves. "Roll 'em down!" the colonel snapped.

While troopers had often dressed casually at Camp Hale, military discipline showed its claws at Camp Swift. Shoes now had to be shined. Ties had to be neatly knotted. Caps had to sit just so. Proper dressing was suddenly important.

Saluting was required. Day by day, the distance widened between officers and men. Morale took another downward plunge. Tempers flared. One day, Sergeant John Campbell was stopped by a private who told him: "Your time is up soon. I'm going to kill you!" (Strangely enough, when the sergeant was later wounded in battle, the same man carried him to safety.) For the first time in the division, some troopers went AWOL. A few of them—those from Texas—disappeared to their hometowns nearby. They had to help bring in the harvest on their parents' farms; labor was scarce. These men soon reappeared at camp.

The Texas outpost had swelled with many Southerners who *could* take the heat. These men were amused by the New Englanders' complaints about insects—praying mantises that looked into windows, mosquitoes whirring overhead during the night—and snakes of all kinds in the desert. Texans were accustomed to this wildlife. The Mountain Troopers' ranks were also joined by Alabama peanut farmers-turned-soldiers. *The Blizzard*, Camp Swift's newspaper, reported the arrival of more men from Tennessee, Kentucky, Georgia, and the Carolinas.

These newcomers had to laugh about *The Blizzard*. Instead of printing "pinup girls" like other army papers, the Mountain Troopers' newspaper displayed a "Pinup Mountain of the Week" on the back page. At night the old troopers would watch color slide shows of Alpine scenes. Word had come from Austin that troopers were seen scaling an eight-floor hotel using ropes. To the amazement of Texans, the climbers had then winged their way down all eight floors by means of a perfect rappel technique. When they ate out, even in the presence of Southerners, the men talked about the ski schools they planned to direct after the war.

All this seemed strange to some new draftees. Their professions—circus riders, rodeo men, ranchers—contrasted with those of the early Tenth Mountain volunteers, who had come from colleges and the ski industry.

The new recruits didn't mind looking after the mules. These mule skinners cleaned and saddled the animals, caught them if they jumped over fences, marched them in parades. The mule skinners fed their charges (about 22 pounds of oats or hay a day) and watered them (18 to 24 gallons each), which turned into a big job. Mules could be ornery and they hated to be tied up. Mules could kick. During September maneuvers, when fighter planes suddenly dived low over the troops, many mules scattered. It took days to catch them. The mule named Hitler went to Camp Swift, too. One of his masters noted in a letter home: "Last week, it took five fellows to lead him around. He's that strong. Today only three men handled him. Some progress! Today they caught Hitler and put blinkers on him. They calmed him some, but he could still buck plenty."

It took many military war games, however, to accustom the beasts to fighter planes zooming down at 300 miles per hour and then—10 feet above the ground—screeching up again. Aside from mules, the division still had 250 horses. A special cavalry unit—one of World War II's last—was mounted on these horses. To ride during maneuvers was much cooler, of course, and so much better than hoofing it.

After Thanksgiving, the division received a new commanding officer who had actually been with the U.S. Cavalry during World War I. He was Brigadier General George P. Hays. Word quickly got around Camp Swift that during one campaign seven horses had been shot out from under the brave general. He had won a Congressional Medal of Honor and a Silver Star, among other decorations.

General Hays had recently been in Casino, Italy, in the thick of one of the most savage battles against the Germans. Earlier he had distinguished himself as a new commander in the D-day assault. After landing at the heavily fortified and defended Omaha Beach, the general had fought in Normandy for 170 days and made a name for himself in the battle for Brest, France. The Tenth Mountain Division took an immediate liking to the slim officer.

The division was going to see a lot of General Hays. He had a nice, honest smile and a modest way about him. Unlike other high-ranking, professional military men, he never boasted and never set himself apart from the soldiers under his command.

General Hays quickly made friends everywhere. And he let the men know it. After getting acquainted with them, he said: "If you're going to risk your life, you might as well do it in good company."

With the arrival of this new commander, the Tenth gradually got its pride back. When a contest was announced to find a nickname for the Tenth Mountain Division, the troopers responded with enthusiasm. Hundreds of names were suggested, and even Colorado civilians sent in their ideas. Among the nicknames suggested were "The Sherpas," "The Timberliners," "The White Devils," "The Conquering Eagles," "General Hays' Huskies," "Hays' Hellcats," and even "Hays' Hellions." Each name brought a fresh wave of pride: "The Mountain Marauders," "The Mountain Lions," "The Mountain Maulers," all told a story. Eventually, the simple term "Mountaineers" won out; the Tenth Mountain Division was finally reborn. Some soldiers who had left the division now wanted to get back in.

General Hays always spoke simply. One day he promised the troops that they would have hard times together. "But also good times," General Hays added. "And we'll soon go into combat."

This caused speculation. Where would the overtrained Mountain Troops finally be sent? Rumors kept making the rounds at camp. Someone was sure that the Tenth would travel to Japanese-held tropical Burma. Others spoke about the Philippines, where General Douglas MacArthur was still fighting inch by inch. On the other hand, General Hays had great knowledge of the war in France, hadn't he? So some "informed" troopers "knew" that the Tenth would shortly take off for western Europe, perhaps to battle in Germany or in Norway's mountains.

The Nazis were now bitterly defending every mile of their home ground. Daily orientation lectures gave the Mountain Troopers an idea about German tactics, German morale, and the German horrors, news of which slowly had seeped out of Europe. According to eyewitnesses, Hitler had set up a devilish murder machine in several occupied countries. One of the worst places was Poland, where Nazi trucks had built-in gassing equipment. Thousands of Jews—men, women, and children—were being picked up by these trucks and killed. Every day about fifteen hundred of these people were being burned and gassed at Auschwitz. Trains brought not only Jews but also Catholic priests, nuns, ministers of the Jehovah's Witnesses, and political dissenters from every occupied country. Only a few of these men and women survived Hitler's death machine. In the meantime, against all rules of war, hundreds of thousands of disarmed Russian prisoners were crammed into huge factory cellars to die from poison gas. Special Nazi units would toss gas pellets through cellar window slits until the crowded, helpless Russians were all dead.

At Camp Swift, such Holocaust news mattered very much indeed. At the Texas post, the Mountain Troops were also shown captured uniforms and motion pictures of various battles.

Something had to happen soon!

CHAPTER
5

This Boat is Going to Italy!

During mid-November 1944, things suddenly began to move. The 86th Regiment received orders to pack all of its gear and supplies. To the men's relief, they were allowed to take their skis, ski poles, ski boots, and other winter equipment. By November 28, everyone in the 86th Mountain Infantry Regiment had pulled out of Camp Swift. The young men did not know their destination, and even if they guessed it, no trooper was permitted to write his family about the four-day trip. It ended in Norfolk, Virginia. A few days after their arrival, several battalions of the 86th, along with some air force boys, boarded the S.S. *Argentina*, which sailed off in a convoy of destroyers.

A few days later the remainder of the 86th Regiment shouldered their winter equipment, along with packs, gas masks, bedrolls, pistol belts, and rifles, and labored up the steep gangplanks of the former S.S. *America*, which had been renamed the U.S.S. *West Point*. After leaving the wintry Virginia coast, the troop ship pushed into the Atlantic with its load of men and material.

During peacetime, each cabin had accommodated two to four people. But with a war on, several tiers of bunk beds reached up to the ceiling. Each cabin now housed twelve to eighteen men, all full of noise and horseplay. Because it was winter, the troops couldn't make use of the decks as sleeping quarters, a custom often observed on Pacific crossings.

The U.S.S. *West Point* tossed in Atlantic waters for several days before the 86th Mountain Regiment finally learned the truth. An officer announced their destination over the public address system: "This boat is going to Italy!"

Almost everyone aboard knew something about Italy. Some former collegians who had actually been there told the other troopers about its magnificent beaches, lovely red-roofed towns shaded by pines, the art treasures of Rome and Florence. All the troopers already knew about the jagged Italian Alps, now occupied by the Germans. Hitler's army had given up Naples and Rome and retreated north to a "Gothic Line" that stretched through the Apennine Mountains. This line was a strong one. It had not given way to several attacks by the U.S. Fifth Army. The Tenth Division was going to be part of this army. Surely, the troopers reasoned, *their* arrival in Italy would change the military picture in the Apennines. From now on the Allied forces would be victorious!

There was much backslapping at the ship's railings.

As the 86th sailed across the Mediterranean and got its first look at the sunny Isle of Capri, other units of the Tenth Mountain Division were leaving Texas. The 85th and 87th spent Christmas and New Year's at Camp Patrick Henry, Virginia. This was known as the East Coast Staging Area. On January 4, 1945, these two regiments also boarded the U.S.S. *West Point*, which had rushed back from Naples for the second load of Mountain Troopers. On the sixth day at sea, a storm arose. The *West Point* rolled and rocked. Water streamed and rushed across the decks. Objects suddenly floated through the holds just below the troop dispensary. Many mountaineers were seasick.

Captain George Earle, official historian for the 87th, re-members what happened next: "Heavy seas tore life rafts through the port side of the ship, pouring tons of seawater into a just vacated bunk. The icy seawater washed gear against the alarmed men as they waded out of bed."

By the time they steamed toward the southern tip of Spain and past the rock of Gibraltar, the Mountaineers were well again. What if the boat docked at Gibraltar and permission was given to climb the rock? Men spoke excitedly about the routes up the famous rock.

The climb was all in their imagination, however, for on January 13, the troop ship docked at Naples. The Italian city had been badly damaged, and the Mountaineers were aston-ished by what Allied bombs could do. To Americans, whose houses stood unharmed from this war, the devastation of the European port left a deep impression. American and British bombs had created havoc with all the buildings fronting the water. B-17s (Flying Fortresses) had made a mess of Na-ples's docks. Some warehouses were reduced to total rubble. Windowpanes had been smashed. Walls gaped with holes. Doors hung askew. Squashed trucks still littered the ground.

To many Mountaineers, it was a first look at war.

The *West Point* had to navigate with great care through the port. In several places masts of half-sunken Italian boats stuck out of the water. Ships' bridges were upside down. Loading ramps floated near collapsed water towers. The coastal section of Kiska had been untouched by comparison with Naples.

War-torn Italy offered other scenes. In the streets of Na-ples, the Mountain Troopers saw flocks of ragged, starving children. Although it was winter, most of them were barefoot or wore old, shabby, oversized shoes. After spending Christmas at Bagnoli, north of Naples, the men of the 86th had seen what war could do to youngsters. There were no children's clothes at all; the young people had to wear cast-off adult jackets and coats and shirts that hung like sacks. Hordes of children begged for food everywhere. Italian adults rummaged through army garbage for potato peelings, old bread crusts, and other leftovers. Used coffee grounds had become precious, and the Italians clamored for salt, sugar— anything edible.

In the northern part of Italy, still occupied by Hitler's troops, even a harvest of apples was shipped to Germany. In January 1945 the northern Italians were reduced to virtual slavery by their former partners. Most of the Italian army, which once fought side by side with Hitler's, had long been disarmed, the Italian generals shot or imprisoned. Since September 1944, Italy's dictator, the proud, flamboyant Benito Mussolini, had been a German puppet, held captive in the Italian lake region, north of the Po Plain.

The cities and farms of the Po River valley felt the occupiers' hard knuckles. The great cities still had to turn out weapons and ammunition for the Hitler war machine. Because agricultural products were confiscated and sent out of Italy, most of the Po farmers were badly off. No Italian could keep so much as a pig, and Fascist bureaucrats counted every onion and ounce of flour. Because of the long war, southern Italy had not much food, either.

The Tenth Mountaineers quickly got into the habit of helping the local population. American soldiers received plenty of canned C rations in Naples for the long journey north. The food cans could be heated on portable stoves. In this way, the troopers transformed the rusty old freight cars into "dining cars," and even "sleeping cars," for each man carried his bedroll. In the daytime, the slow freight train be-

Maj. Gen. George P. Hays looks out over the Po Valley and watches his division spread out into the valley.
(U.S. Army photograph)

came an observation train, for there were many foreign sights —"two-wheel horse carts, narrow streets, upper windows with balconies, women carrying large bundles on their heads —" as one sergeant of the 86th remarked. In Pisa the troopers saw the famous Leaning Tower. The 86th dug its foxholes and set up its tents not far from the Tower, directly under dark-green pines. But soon the 86th traveled farther north and even closer to the front lines. The 85th had reached Pisa from Naples by sea, on infantry landing crafts. The First Battalion of the 87th made part of the journey on a tiny freighter, switching to trucks in Livorno (Leghorn).

All the Mountaineers were shocked by Italy's poverty. In the north the Germans were the masters and therefore lacked for nothing. Their heavy-jowled supreme commander, Field Marshal Albert Kesselring, was a good example. He always looked splendid, with a suntanned face and a sturdy body. Despite his frequent smiles, which earned him the American nickname "Smiling Al," Kesselring was a tough man. He had first won Hitler's respect as a *Luftwaffe* (air force) commander, who dropped some of World War II's first bombs on Warsaw, Poland. That country's surrender came fast. Kesselring had also smashed all resistance in Holland by bombing. Even as peace discussions with the small country went on, Kesselring gave orders to burn down Rotterdam from the air. The town had no flak defense and the destruction brought Holland to its knees. Kesselring defeated Belgium in the same manner and then flew to North Africa, where he assisted General Erwin Rommel. When U.S. forces landed at Salerno, it was Field Marshal Kesselring—now commanding ground forces—who almost tossed the Americans into the sea. He was as able a general as he was brutal with civilians.

The Tenth Mountaineers were beginning to hear a great deal about Kesselring and his forces. The field marshal's position, north of Pisa, was an excellent one. The German Fourth Corps consisted of about twenty-five divisions. Some of these were deeply entrenched in the spine of the Apennines hills. German panzer (armored) units controlled the few roads. Some of the terrain was rutted by narrow paths snaking in and out of ravines and up and down hillsides. German pillboxes made any assault a bloody undertaking. Kesselring's well-trained veterans could range their mortars on anyone coming closer than 600 feet. Heavy German artillery sat snugly in the granite terrain. After abandoning Rome and giving away Florence, the German army was planning to hold on to these hills. Their position was strong enough for Kesselring to boast to a fellow officer: "The Americans must realize that they're hopelessly lost against the German might."

The Allies were now superior in the air, for much of Hermann Göring's *Luftwaffe* had been shot down. However, despite this advantage and excellent support from the U.S. Navy, the Allies were at a standstill in front of Kesselring's Gothic Line. Snow lay across the hillsides. From one Italian coast to the other, all across the mountain range, the two mighty forces remained in villages opposite one another, waiting for the winter thaws, so that they could rip each other to pieces. General Sir Harold Alexander, Allied Commander in Chief in Italy, and General Mark Clark, U.S. Commander in Chief, had perhaps the more complicated task. The Allied army consisted of twenty-eight different nationalities, including British, Australians, South Africans, French, Poles, a Jewish brigade from Palestine, Brazilians, and Americans. Kesselring commanded mostly Germans, plus a small remnant of the Italian army and some White Russians.

Kesselring faced one major obstacle. In recent years the bitter, starved Italians had banded together into *partigiani*, partisan units. These civilian fighters received arms from the Allies, mostly from the Americans.

Italian partisans always struck swiftly and then withdrew into the hills. Like the Finns, these natives knew their country, and they made life miserable for Kesselring. A small convoy was ambushed. A German fell, riddled by bullets while on his way to buy eggs. Sometimes, instead of making war on the Germans, the partisans worked for the Allies. They hid shot-down Allied bomber pilots and helped Americans with their maps.

Before reaching the front lines, the Mountain Troopers had a chance to talk to some of these partisans. The *partigiani* were tightly organized, fanatic and fearless, and they knew what they were doing.

Their anger dictated each day's action. They had become especially infuriated by a Kesselring announcement that the "fight against the partisans has to be carried out with all means available and the utmost severity." The previous June,

Kesselring had also said: "I shall defend any one of my leaders who in his choice of methods goes beyond the usual normal reserve. The principle must be that it is better to make a mistake in the choice of means than it is to be neglectful and careless in carrying out this assignment."

This meant, of course, that German troops could—and would frequently—fire on any innocent civilian caught in the hills at the wrong time. It also meant that Italians could have their fingernails torn out by Kesselring's Gestapo. Tenth Mountaineers were soon to hear of partisans who had all their teeth knocked out, whose bones had been smashed by hammers, and those who had been hung upside down in cellars for days. After these tortures, Italian freedom fighters were often shot.

Strangely enough, none of these measures got results. Oppressed men often fight all the harder. So the partisans continued harassing their foe wherever they could.

A short time before the Tenth Mountain Division moved toward the front lines, Kesselring gave a final warning. He told the local population: "From now on . . . we will act in the most severe manner. . . . People who help the partisans will be hanged in the public square. Villages will be burned and destroyed."

Such brutality was ammunition for the Allies, and General Hays made sure to inform his troops about the enemy they were facing. As the U.S. Army's only mountain division, the Tenth was eager to come to grips with Kesselring's forces. The latter would soon be aware of the 85th, 86th, 87th, and the supporting regiments. "We conquer mountains and men" was still their motto.

6

First Combat: "Hungry and Lean, but Our Rifles are Clean"

The 86th was first to see action. The regiment got its baptism of fire near Cutigliano and Orsigna on January 8, 1945. As part of the Fifth Army's Task Force 45, each mountain battalion moved to a different location, but all the troopers soon heard the rumbling sound of German artillery.

At night the Mountaineers could see the flashes of German guns lighting up the sky. To start with, being in the rear, the 86th drew little blood. Their introduction to war was quiet enough that January. There were marches, hikes, and patrols on skis. There was guard duty amid mud and snow. So far, the snow still hadn't been reddened.

In the Apennines hills just then, living conditions could have been worse. The Mountaineers were often billeted with Italian families, who made every effort to please. According to one sergeant, the Third Battalion of the 86th was often invited into Italian homes to share the wine and "to marvel at their old kettles, tables, and chairs." The Battalion Command Post was set up in a former sanatorium. Furnaces didn't lack wood, and candles or gas lanterns gave enough light to study war maps. "We felt very brave for not paying much attention to the artillery," someone wrote later.

The men would long remember their first impression of these Italian hills, white with snow and peppered by red-roofed villages, the mountains themselves lovely to look at. But these were surface views; reality was harsher. That winter had plenty of ice to slip on, deep mud to sink into, cold wet snows. Men stumbled in the darkness, and Italian scouts

struggled with snowshoes, sometimes falling down. One battalion tried horses, but they were useless. Whenever the Germans sent a shell in their direction, the riders had to jump off. In general, the Apennine roads were so poor that no truck —not even a jeep—could move on them. Supplies came by burro. Some of the daytime reconnaissance was done on skis. Skis made it possible to cross the frozen rivers, to claw upward through deep drifts that would otherwise reach to a man's shoulders. Skis made it possible to get away fast, especially if the escape route led downhill. The white skis blended with the snow. When they stood still, troopers could hardly be seen in their white parkas and white poles. If he moved in close to the enemy, though, a trooper had to remove his skis. Wood made a clattering sound; walking was quieter. The Germans used the same tactics and their troopers were also camouflaged.

The 85th Regiment had left Pisa on January 20. It was now scattered over the gentle hillsides. The First Battalion, under Colonel Donald Wooley, had its headquarters at Bagni di Lucca, a good-sized town. The other battalions of the 85th spread into places with names as musical and beautiful as the Italian language itself: Limestre, Gavinana, Prunetta. "The entire sector for the regiment was a quiet one," noted one officer. "No major engagements."

Just the same, the 87th Regiment got its own sniff of the front. According to the 87th official history, the first shot against the enemy was fired the morning of January 27. The unit had waited four years for this "resounding bang" against the German forces. The shells crashed out of nine pack howitzers as a "warm-up" exercise.

The next day, eighteen mortars from the weapons companies were emplaced and fired. On the 29th and 30th, sixty riflemen from the 87th First and Third Battalions went on sniping missions in the mountainous terrain just inland from the coast, northeast of Seravezza. Like all regiments, the 87th set out on many nightly patrols over frigid ground.

Patrols assembled about 7 P.M. near the 87th's positions at Camaiore, Villa Colli, and Valpromaro. Plans were discussed with the sergeants, maps were studied, *partigiani* were consulted. Everything had to be clear. The men quickly learned that each reconnaissance outing gave the troopers a chance to answer questions: What is the terrain like? Has the enemy moved? What are the Germans up to? Which are the German units? (The Tenth Mountain patrols tried to take prisoners whenever possible. The prisoners of war would then be questioned by Intelligence Officers.)

The men of the 87th were dressed for the chilly night in their long parkas, sweaters, and heavy underwear. They wore GI gloves but left their helmets behind. A helmet scraping a tree banch would give the show away.

After a last hot cup of coffee, each man took his battle-ready M-1 rifle, weighing about 10 pounds. The rifle clip yielded eight shots. Some patrols had as many as fifty troopers, others required only twelve to fifteen. In the 87th, a few night patrols were kept down to six to eight men. Among them they carried two Thompson submachine guns that could fire rapidly.

Smoking was forbidden. If the Germans saw the slightest flame, they would send up a flare and then rake the terrain with machine guns, twenty bullets per second, twelve hundred bullets a minute. The troopers also had to learn the night's password which was changed every night. This would enable them to get back into their own lines. L Company, 87th, used "Red Fox" at least once.

Upon their return at dawn, the 87th patrol leader would say: "Red Fox!"

Immediately, the L Company guard would answer: "Blue Velvet!"

The troopers were in the clear then. They could come home again.

Some Tenth Mountain patrols were preceded by specialists of the 126th Mountain Engineer Battalion, who had to check the paths for mines. This was called sapping. It was always dangerous work. The engineer would move a mine detector ahead of him. This gadget looked like a vacuum cleaner. On many occasions, the sappers themselves were blown up by the mines; at other times, the engineers could pave the way for the troopers by using sticks of dynamite on the mines. The first Tenth Mountain casualties were seven men and a chaplain from the 86th. They were killed when they stepped on a "shoe" mine that lay hidden under the snow. Such "antipersonnel" mines were as small as a package of cigarettes. If a man put his weight on one, he would be blown up.

Patrols faced other kinds of mines as well. The German "Bouncing Betty" startled everyone with a spring that flung the exploding mine as high as a man's hips. There were mines that could be tripped by wires; an explosion occurred as soon as anyone touched the wire. For this reason, night patrols went about with broom handles that could be waved in front of each man as he walked. When no brooms were available, a small willow branch would do. There had to be quite a distance between the troopers in case of explosions or enemy bombardment.

After a few days' experience, the troopers gained a special feel; they could grope about them gently with their hands. A man thus learned the location of a trip wire. Then he could step over it and whisper a warning to those who followed him. In time, infantrymen were sufficiently trained to disarm these killers.

At least one corporal made the claim that he could actually "smell" the presence of a living person. It was vital to listen to every sound. One patrol leader later wrote in his diary: "That first trip out into the great unknown land of the enemy can be more nerve-racking to the individual than the mass movements of battle. There is the long strain of silent movement, the breathless waits, the searching out of him who lies in waiting to kill. There is the physical punishment and even torture of alternately sweating up the rough terrain and lying motionless for hours on the snow . . . freezing in your own icy sweat."

It was important to look hard, to see every flitting white-clothed, ghostly shadow, to hear every rustle in the bushes. Footprints in the snow counted, as did a knowledge of German. On some patrols, interpreters could hear others talking among themselves.

The enemy was clever. Some Germans spoke English. They would call, "Is that you, Joe?"

If an American answered, the shooting began from the other side. Captain George Earle, 87th, was fascinated by the "hotbed of flashing lights, green and blue flares, skulking figures on ridges and assorted shots. . . ."

Patrols were often hampered by weather. In early February the Apennines chain turned icy cold. On one mission almost every gun jammed on the subzero peaks, and Tenth Mountain men remembered Camp Hale's "D" Series. An Apennine field message between patrol and headquarters concluded: "Very high wind. Visibility poor. Snow is knee- to waist-deep. Could not see Monte Spigolino. Had to dig foot-holds to timber. Crampons and ice axes needed badly. . . ."

By and large, the front was a static one on all sectors. The Tenth Mountain troopers still hadn't seen fierce fighting.

Meanwhile, the war in this mountain range was fought on an almost humane basis. On occasion, the Germans would wait to bang away with their artillery until the Americans started something first. If a Mountain Trooper was hurt in a riflemen's skirmish, Kesselring's soldiers might even give him first aid until the American medics could come and get him. And despite Kesselring's stern warning that all farmers must get out of the area or be "shot as spies," some of the Italians still stayed in their homes.

It could happen that an old stone building and the family barns were on different sides of the front. In between was no-man's-land where shots could be traded. One Italian farm woman managed to cross from her house to her stables. An hour later, despite the Germans and the Americans, she was back again with a bucket of milk. This practice, decided one American officer, was not in the best interests of the Allied endeavor. The farmer was going to follow orders from now on just like a soldier. According to a coded message from one company of the 87th to another: "Woman going through our lines to milk cow will have to bring cow back to our side!"

Because they had reached the front before other regiments, the men of the 86th could now go on a brief furlough to Florence, 30 miles south. Here one could see the cathedrals and magnificent statues and the world's most famous paintings. Here was the Ponte Vecchio, an old bridge filled with jewelry stores that sold souvenirs. Here were medieval castles and magnificent parks of cypresses. Old friends could be found among the uniformed men on leave and new friends could be made. There was wine and there were women who liked the Mountaineers. But the relaxation never lasted; after a few days, they had to go back to the front and other men took their places on a brief holiday.

Both sides were waiting for the big battle. They gathered their strength, their equipment, their ammunition. Both awaited their opportunity. The U.S. Fifth Army was massing some 270,000 men. Of these, about fourteen thousand belonged to the Tenth Mountain Division, which was supported by three field artillery battalions, an antitank battalion, a medical battalion, a quartermaster battalion, the ordnance, military police, and the mountain signal unit.

But foot soldiers of the 85th, 86th, and 87th regiments were always up front. Many patrols later, the Tenth Division would show that it was as good as one of its songs:

> The roughest, the toughest, we're dirty and mean
> Hungry and lean, but our rifles are clean—

Soon the rifles would move upward to make the Tenth a legend.

7

Riva Ridge is for Mountaineers

By early February 1945 an important decision had been made in Italy. Of all Allied troops facing the Germans, there was only one logical division to spearhead through enemy lines. Only the Tenth Mountain Division would be able to bore a hole into Field Marshal Kesselring's troops. Only specialized mountain warfare would change the difficult situation.

Every hill between Bologna and a point 24 miles north of Florence was still in German hands. Germans sat on strategically crucial peaks, on Monte Serrasicca, on Pizzo di Campiano, on Monte Belvedere and Monte Gorgolesco and Monte della Torraccia, and on dozens of others. The Germans had had even more time to dig in deeply, to build more fortresses for themselves, even to use concrete and steel. They were safe in their bunkers and their pillboxes. Some twenty-five divisions strong, they were well supplied with machine guns and had enough artillery to destroy anyone who tried to drive them out. And there were good soldiers manning these outposts. They were always alert for the Americans, as well as the British and the Brazilians, who fought beside them. Field Marshal Kesselring predicted that the Allies would not get through. And for five months, he had been right. He had been a formidable enemy, and American units hadn't budged his Gothic Line.

But the Tenth Mountain Division, in Italy now for just a few weeks, would change all that. Major General George P. Hays realized that the moment had come for his men. They knew the terrain, and they were ideally suited for it.

General Hays himself was installed in a mountain town named San Marcello, to the northwest of Pistoia. There, behind high walls and a screen of sentries, in a villa once owned by an Italian admiral, General Hays concentrated on the forthcoming battle. Every day he received more Intelligence reports from his German-speaking interrogators of prisoners of war. Every day there were more detailed aerial maps of the region.

Where should the blow fall? For General Hays and his superior, Lieutenant General Lucian K. Truscott, Fifth Army Commander, the choice soon narrowed to two objectives.

One was 3,876-foot Monte Belvedere, which sits like a long, gently sloping pear above the little villages of Vidiciatico and Querciola. German Grenadier units controlled the five miles of ascent through winter-shrouded wheat and barley fields and through bushes. It would be a long way to the summit, but not a steep one. General Truscott definitely wanted to start with Monte Belvedere.

General Hays favored another mountain. This was Pizzo di Campiano, with its rocky, perpendicular Riva Ridge. "Riva is far tougher," General Hays said. "The Germans would never believe that anyone can scale it!"

At first, the two generals couldn't agree. "That cliff seems impossible," General Hays kept saying. "But Riva is the key to the Monte Belvedere."

General Hays finally persuaded his superior that Riva Ridge would protect the flanks of other Tenth Mountain units who would climb Belvedere a day later. The Tenth Mountain Division would become famous for its ascent.

As a prelude, in early February, the First Battalion of the 86th Regiment was mysteriously whisked away from the lines. In the big transport trucks, the troops were driven to Lucca, west of Pistoia, and about a mile east of the ocean beaches. The men wanted to know what was going on.

At last, an officer from General Hays' headquarters appeared. He brought with him a wax model of Campiano mountain, with its Riva Ridge, in all its toothlike sharpness. The model also showed Monte Belvedere, to the east, which would become the combat province for the 85th and 87th regiments of the Tenth Mountain Division. The Fifth Army had failed several times to take and hold Belvedere.

But Riva would be the most dangerous, the officer admitted. Allied planes couldn't help because the Germans must not be alerted. There could not even be artillery support, for the enemy would know at once that an attack was coming if the big U.S. guns started pounding. Riva was too steep for jeeps, and no tanks could ever get up there. On the summit sat elements of the Germans' 232nd Grenadier Division, IV Corps.

So it would be the men against this sheer, stony mountain, and against the German garrison on top. Only the best Mountaineers could make it.

Not one of the assembled members of the 86th wanted to be left out of the battle. They were itching for action. Fortunately, in the next two weeks, the troopers had to test their mettle against a rugged Lucca marble quarry. The rock faces were as high as buildings. Instructors made the men scale these rocks for many hours, just as they had done at Camp Hale—up, up, up those ropes, then down again, then up once more. This was a fine refresher course, and at the end of it, most of the men felt strong. One of them wrote his mother: "Nothing can faze us now. We've trained all those years. We've polished it off with more training. We're in top form and ready for anything!" A sergeant, who was later wounded, told an army reporter, "I feel so strong now I can dodge bullets, I want to go into battle." The battalion also concentrated on rifle shooting, despite all the practice they had had at Camps Hale and Swift.

By mid-February, the Riva specialists were back in the big Apennines hills. To the Germans, U.S. life in the red-roofed villages must have appeared quieter than ever. Nothing much happened during the day; all American troop movements— and patrols—still took place at night, under the cover of darkness.

Finally, February 18 dawned cold and yellow. Down in the stone houses, the men of the 86th stirred, and all day long the tension rose at the base of the ridge. In Vidiciatico, one edge of which stares straight into the stony eye of Riva, and in Lizzano, on another hill, the men sat in houses and waited. Sergeant Andrew Gordon, Second Battalion, 86th, and his platoon spent the sunlit day in a church. From time to time, they aimed their field glasses at Riva Ridge, which they could spy through the slit of the belfry.

Sergeant Gordon noticed that the Riva summit was still snow-covered. Icy patches glinted in the light, and some of the most treacherously jutting rocks were blue with ice because of the shade. The rock experts gave Riva their full attention. Where would it be safest to go up at night? Which were the best spots for the nail-like pitons that would hold the ropes? Each piton point had to be picked with perfection; the life of many soldiers would depend on every rope. What if one of the rock holds pulled out and the men fell to their deaths? In the houses, the troopers carefully inspected their nylon ropes; the khaki strands had to be without flaws. A small cut could send several climbers to their death. The pitons received another inspection. All rusty steel was thrown away. Only the freshest, newest pitons would be used.

In the afternoon the men checked and oiled other equipment. Their M-1 rifles had to be clean and ready. Their two bandoliers of ammunition had to be intact. Before evening, the climbers readied their packs. Each man carried a two-day supply of cold rations, a filled canteen, a shovel for digging foxholes, two blankets, and first-aid supplies. The men knew it wouldn't be easy to get the wounded off the steep mountain towers.

By 8 P.M. it was dark enough to walk out of the houses and into the night. There would be no moon. The sky was clear and cold. In the church the sergeant blew out the candles over which his platoon had cooked one last warm meal. On the mountain no lights would be permitted.

The men had to use their memories and trust their good luck. They slowly stepped forward on the dark trails. They kept their distance, so that they wouldn't whip tree branches into one another's faces. They walked slowly to avoid dislodging stones. No one spoke. Any noise might set the powerful German searchlights in motion; and the mortars and machine guns were never far behind. Everyone realized that if the 86th failed to take Riva, many days would be lost for Belvedere, too. It was one of the war's gambles.

A mishap occurred on the tiny Dardagna River. Suddenly, three men stumbled and fell, because the water was studded with slick boulders not visible in the darkness. No one drowned in the cold, belly-high river, but one Mountaineer was wet to his waist. He had to change quickly. His buddies only got wet feet.

Higher up, Mountain Troopers crunched across the first snow. This meant a little more light. For about 50 yards, the snow offered some landmarks—they recognized a large rock, a clump of trees, a steep slope of cobbles. All at once, the whiteness ended and every upward step was guesswork again. Not every climber could remember all the features of Riva, and a few men lost their bearings. One sergeant who had devoted a whole Sunday to a field-glass study of Riva now couldn't find his route at all. He led his men through deep brush and bushes and trees, across a slope of tiny, unstable stones that might have brought everyone crashing down but didn't, and finally, onto a wall that had few wedges for climbing hardware.

One company was fortunate; it had been their lot to use Riva's one and only trail for the night adventure. For almost everyone else, the grueling task of battling a thousand feet of rock began. This was the steep face, the monster face they had studied from below. This was the heart of Riva, and the most harrowing part of the climb. The best Mountaineers—

Supported from the air by fighter-bombers, 10th Mountain Division men on the Porretta-Moderna Highway in Della Vedetta, Italy, fire on Germans about 200 yards away.
(U.S. Army photograph)

the rock vanguards—went ahead, their rifle slings tight, their hardware clicking around their belts, their ropes ready to be installed for those who followed. But as the first men edged upward to install the pitons that would hold the rings for the ropes, there was a surprise. The rock proved more brittle than they had thought. The spikes were driven in, but a pulling test brought bad news; the steel came out again. New wedges and slits had to be found, and the padded hammers had to be used carefully, sparingly, with a dull click, click. Would the Germans be able to hear this work on the mountain? What if a German sentry suddenly looked down and saw an approaching army of Mountaineers?

But nothing stirred on the summit, and the support points, once firm, held well as the troops climbed, single file, up the perpendicular stone. If anyone panicked, if anyone got stuck and couldn't move and shouted, the whole show would be given away. But not a word was said, and the steady procession went on.

Some columns were far ahead of others. One of the leaders was Lieutenant Colonel Henry Hampton, who had been a fire chief in civilian life. A superb athlete, he had great physical strength and stamina. As an officer, he now inspired others. Another of the many upward-driving, scrambling, eager columns was led by Colonel Clarence Tomlinson, who had already made a name for himself through his bravery in battle. The colonel was known to walk, stand, and run through any shelling when everyone else crawled. Furthermore, he had often placed his headquarters so far ahead that the German artillery, instead of killing this officer, fired straight over him. Scaling the mountain with the colonel was Sergeant Torger Tokle, one of the world's best ski jumpers. Despite the great danger, the summit drew all these men like a magnet.

They were hardly aware of their heavy packs, which pulled each climber downward and backward. Every man also carried a hundred rounds of ammunition, which could explode if hit.

Yet there was no fire at all. The Germans were still unaware that hundreds of Americans kept inching their way up to their "impregnable" fortress. ("No one could climb that!" a German later observed. "It was like a castle wall!")

The "castle" was getting colder and icier with every passing hour. By two in the morning, some of the climbers had reached the most difficult rocks. These were covered with verglas, a hard, slippery ice, which is always bothersome on glaciers. One column even encountered a frozen waterfall, but somehow they bypassed it. So far, none of the troopers had fallen. There were no accidents, only some bad moments. At one point, in the total blackout, a sergeant reached out too far on the rock. Soon he couldn't move his arms or feet. He hung on, spread-eagled, until a climber behind him came to his assistance and found the right holds for his feet.

By morning, a slight haze hung over Riva, and more men could edge upward without being seen. Still no shot had been fired.

Then at dawn, a German sentry saw one of the First Mountain Troopers. The German's mouth fell open. He raised his arms. Later, he said: "I thought I was seeing ghosts."

Then another GI appeared and strode forward. Suddenly he tripped. He had stumbled over a German wire that gave the alarm inside the bunker. Immediately, the defenders burst to life. Submachine gun ablaze, an officer came racing out of the dugout.

But the fight was brief. The Mountain Troopers charged him, and the hand grenades sailed into the German installation. Panzer Grenadiers soon hurried out, in a gesture of surrender. The defenders were so outnumbered that they willingly gave up.

While the prisoners were taken down the easy trail, other members of the 86th combed the German position. The quarters were comfortable ones, with genuine bunk beds, pictures of sweethearts on the walls, and even an old phonograph on the floor. The soldiers also found German black bread, canned butter, and candy.

A little later, to their astonishment, the Tenth Mountaineers looked into the eyes of fifty more Germans. They had been sent up to relieve their comrades and found the Americans instead. It was another almost bloodless surrender. Would it be this easy on Monte Belvedere?

8

Belvedere: He Who Commands the Heights

General George P. Hays issued a simple field order for the night of February 19, 1945: "The Tenth Mountain Division will attack . . . to seize, occupy, organize, and defend Mt. Belvedere, and prepare for action to the northeast. . . ." These sparse military lines could not tell the whole story, which was underlined by General Mark Clark, Fifth Army: "Mt. Belvedere must be captured before we can advance. . . ."

Like other Apennine peaks, Monte Belvedere controlled several of the highways leading north. It was one of the gates to northern Italy. If Belvedere was taken, U.S. troops could finally smash into the rich plains of the Po River, into the larder of Europe. If the Germans were driven from the summit, it would be possible to free the big cities—Bologna, Milan, Verona, Venice—and ram still farther north, toward the borders of Switzerland. World War II could be nearing its end.

Here was the Tenth Mountain Division's great chance, for all the officers knew that Monte Belvedere was a tough target. It had resisted Allied troops again and again. The reasons were summed up in a military rule: "He who holds the heights commands the battlefield."

On top of Belvedere, the Germans sat in deep, straight ditches that ran across the whole summit. German 50-mm mortars, known as *Granatwerfer*, as well as German machine guns, submachine guns, and rifles, could be swiveled toward an attacker. Large German howitzer artillery could upset any convoys that might dare drive through the valleys. German hand grenades, flung by the seasoned men of the 1044 Regiment, 232 Division, could silence anyone with enough nerve to crawl up to Belvedere. Every ravine and gully was under the defender's scrutiny.

The vast acreage was also heavily mined. Mines blocked the major trails that led uphill. Mines barred the one road that could have been used by U.S. tanks. The Germans often planted plastic or ceramic mines that could not be detected by mine sweeping equipment, which only picks up metal. Once when the U.S. engineers put on their earphones and listened, there was a horrible noise: an engineer had stepped on a mine. Plastics just didn't register. Sometimes, too, the enemy had put up signs reading, ACHTUNG! MINEN! where they had nothing at all. It was a confusing and dangerous business.

Italians had been blown up by mines, too. For over a year now Monte Belvedere had been combed by brave local citizens who wanted to help the Americans. These partisans searched the sloping fields and the olive groves for German gun installations. The Italians crept up in the dead of night, seeking out the locations of barbed wires, looking for German trenches and German units, and preparing information for U.S. Intelligence and American artillery. Any Italian civilian caught in these acts could expect the worst. He was likely to be tortured by the enemy's secret police, and then shot. On Belvedere, a partisan leader named Antonio Giurido was killed by the Germans, who then attached a small unseen bomb to his body. When other Italian fighters came to get their dead chief, they were also blown up.

Partisans acted as scouts. This was risky, too, because the scout—as the first man on a U.S. patrol—would be first in the firing line when the Germans discovered a patrol. More often than not, the scout would be a U.S. sergeant or corporal of the Tenth Mountain Division. For a month now, all action of the 86th and 87th regiments had taken place at night. In the darkness, scouts had to walk carefully, their hands and feet acting like antennas against the many trip wires that set off mines. "Don't step on it," they would whisper to one another during a patrol. "Careful, careful." One corporal of the 87th was said to keep his hands in front of him "like a blind man." It was always startling when a finger touched a trip wire. Moving the finger just another inch meant setting off an explosion that might kill the whole platoon. Some U.S. patrols had used police dogs from the canine corps. One night the lead dog fell into a German foxhole. As luck would have it, he promptly jumped out again, and then, just before the sentries started shooting, he led the soldiers back to their units.

How many lives would Belvedere cost, the staff officers asked themselves? How many men would get through? Was one night sufficient to scale the summit? Could they buy enough time to go undetected? Once there, would it be possible to hold Belvedere? Even ten hours before the attack, no one was sure of every angle.

On the morning of February 19, General Hays's Mountain Troopers were as ready as they would ever be. They had much in their favor. Units of the 86th were hanging on to Riva Ridge. Thus, the Germans could not fire from that direction. Moreover, the Belvedere men had great physical strength.

Having been in Italy just a month, they were fresh and eager and confident, with a tremendous fighting spirit and great pride in their outfit.

During the morning of the 19th, officers and the men of the 85th and 87th regiments filled every house in every nearby mountain village. The units were so well hidden that enemy Intelligence never had a warning of the coming night assault.

Six more hours!

That afternoon a few troopers wrote a last letter home. Others played cards. Some noncommissioned officers eagerly studied their 5-mile route up the peak. Toward evening, weapons were inspected. The Tenth Mountain Artillery had readied about 155 howitzers of 75-mm caliber. Mortars were well concealed under the netting and trees. In the village stables, especially in Vidiciatico, American mules waited side by side with the much tinier Italian mules. The American pack animals had voyaged here all the way from Texas. Italian partisans were already loading the howitzers and supplies as the men stood by. Everywhere, fresh ammunition was being issued.

The medics received their last-minute supply of bandages and morphine. Already wearing their Red Cross–marked helmets, the medics counted their stretchers. In all, some ten thousand soldiers would be on the move that night.

Three more hours!

Once more, General Hays briefed his staff at headquarters, which had been moved closer to the battle scene. Field glasses raised, the top officers studied the approach again. Among those who were to make the fateful decisions that night were Brigadier General David Ruffner, Brigadier General Robinson Duff, and Colonel Earl La Due.

Before they set out, the troopers had a last warm meal. On the mountain no fires could be made. In fact, no one would even be allowed to smoke. Last minute orders: the night climb had to be silent. No one was to speak. No trooper could fire his rifle until the officers gave the signal. Artillery would be used only at the last moment.

By 11 P.M. the attack was cocked. Singly and in pairs, the men had filed out of the houses, from behind walls, from fox-holes, tents, stables, barns. Many of the troops marched from Vidiciatico, but others came from Querciola, Lizzano, Gaggio Montano. All the earth-colored, tile-roofed villages stirred with Mountain Troopers. The groups were kept small, so as not to arouse suspicion. No trucks were used; they made handy targets. Each company was strung out, single file, broken down into tiny columns of men. The distance from soldier to soldier was about 10 yards.

Here and there Italian women materialized out of the night. Black shawls over their heads, the women squeezed the young troopers' hands. The Italians had every reason to wish for the Americans to succeed. The local people wanted to be free of the Germans once and for all. The previous September 27, after a single, stray shot was fired by a Vidiciatico civilian, the *Wehrmacht* (German soldiers) had rushed into innocent homes and killed grandmothers and little children, forty in all. Vidiciatico now thirsted for revenge.

By 11:30 P.M., the First Battalion of the 87th had reached the remaining houses of La Corona; they were directly across from Riva Ridge, which was well covered by the First Battalion of the 86th. Using many back roads, the Third Battalion of the 86th started up adjacent Monte Gorgolesco. The Third Battalion of the 85th, considered one of the most important, began its direct ascent of Monte Belvedere. The officers chose the shortest, most direct route. It also proved the most dangerous.

The climbers were all in excellent condition. Fatigue did not exist for these young men, who now pushed upward like ants. Most of the men were heavily loaded, with three to five hand grenades clipped to their gun belts, rifles, and filled packs.

As the young men moved uphill, the night turned colder. The ground was hard and frozen, and little could be seen. No moon shone. Now and then, a trooper would suddenly fall into a hole. The mountain had been bombarded heavily during the past month leaving many craters. In one valley, a U.S. artificial smoke-making machine sent up a cottony flag of fog, just in case the Germans switched on their searchlights.

For units of the 85th Regiment, everything went according to plan. They scrambled up yard by yard, undiscovered. The First Battalion of the 87th was not that lucky. A few minutes after midnight, one of the companies drew fire from a pillbox. German burp guns—submachine guns—and 88-mm artillery suddenly roared through the night. This drew artillery fire from U.S. positions in the valleys.

Some platoons which had edged upward behind scout dogs were now in trouble. The dogs started barking, giving away their positions. Almost immediately, artillery started booming from all sides: the Germans against the Americans, the Americans against the Germans.

At about the same time, several hundred men of the Second Battalion, 87th, got lost in a minefield. Each mine detonation made fierce lights in the night. On another mountain, men of the First Brazilian Division, some of them with sacks of grenades on their backs, also stumbled into the mines. Explosions kept rocking the ground, and the Latin Americans began to stampede. Many of them died.

From Riva Ridge, which now had been in Allied hands for about twenty-eight hours, Mountain Troopers of the 86th observed the weird flashes and the pounding guns all over Belvedere and the surrounding mountains. It was a little like the Fourth of July. The men had a ringside seat for the fireworks, but so far they could do nothing to help. By now, many of the Signal Corps wires that connected various units with headquarters had been destroyed by artillery. Most companies were cut off. The 86th on Riva still didn't know whether their comrades had climbed to the top of Belvedere.

The 85th was indeed inching up and, oddly enough, was still safe. All the while, other Tenth Mountaineers were stepping onto mines. Midway up Belvedere, in a gully, platoon sergeant Dick Wilson had half his arm ripped off by mortar fire. The medics applied a tourniquet and stopped the worst flow of blood. While the battle burned all around, first-aid men gave the sergeant a shot of morphine against the terrible pain. He staggered downhill, miraculously crossing a mine-field without further damage. Two hours later, his arm still hanging in rags, Wilson got to a field hospital in an old farm-house. It was promptly shelled, but Wilson survived.

Despite heavy injuries, morale proved strong. When some-one was wounded, he often wept more because he hated to

A white-clad combat patrol of the 10th Mountain Division crosses near the crest of strategic Mt. Belvedere.
(U.S. Army photograph)

leave his unit and his friends than because of pain. There were so many wounded that medics eventually ran out of stretchers. They transported men on old doors taken from nearby farmhouses. They used weasels, the tracked white vehicles that could maneuver on snow, and small sleds. In the din of battle, the 126th Engineers tried to put up their ingenious tramway for the wounded. It was a difficult job during the German mortar fire, because shell fragments sliced the engineers' cables. But the unit kept working, and before the night was over, their elevator functioned. Captain Fred A. Nagel—the man who had strung the cable and was responsible for its operation—was well-equipped for the task. He was an engineer in civilian life. At dawn, his platoons had their hands full of emergency cases.

Yet for every wounded man, two dozen others headed upward toward the goal. Many squads remained unhurt and intact, and there was no sense of exhaustion. Most of the troopers didn't even feel any fear. The Tenth Mountain Division had been trained for just such a night.

Before dawn, the 85th Regiment received unexpected help.

British Royal Air Force Spitfires swept through the sky. They were joined by several P-47 planes of the U.S. Air Force. One after another, the planes swooped down as smoothly as birds of prey to strafe German positions with great accuracy. In radio contact with Tenth Mountain headquarters, the air armada left a trail of smoke. "It was like a Hollywood movie," a Mountain Trooper later said. "It was perfect timing."

As the craft disappeared, many of the troopers cheered loudly. On top of Belvedere, at least one of the German positions was now silent. It had been blasted with several small rockets. Would anyone up there still be alive? Another pilot, at work on another peak, wrote later in his report: "One bomb near hit—building demolished. Remainder of bombs within target area. Five or six Germans fleeing from buildings. Three or four killed. Observed flashes from mortar in another area. To soldier lying in hole, harassed by artillery, sight of diving plane, flash of rockets, and tremendous bomb blast was a heartening one." But the enthusiasm of another pilot got out of hand: He dropped a bomb on a building full of Americans.

Before the sun had come up, the Third Battalion of the 85th Regiment was on top of Belvedere. The First Battalion, 87th, moving up from another direction, was not far behind.

On the summit, Kesselring's outnumbered soldiers tried a trick. They emerged from their dugouts with hands raised. Several Tenth Mountaineers stepped forward. But it was a fake surrender. Suddenly, the "prisoners of war" hit the ground. Behind them, more Germans started firing their machine guns. "Company C took no further prisoners of war," ran the U.S. report that morning.

On Riva, the desperate defenders had also made a counterattack, using another trick. These soldiers had dressed like medics and run up with covered stretchers. In amazement, the Americans had seen the "medics" tear the blankets off their stretchers. On them were machine guns. But the phony first-aid men never had a chance to use them.

There was action on all mountaintops. The First Battalion of the 85th, under command of Lieutenant Colonel Donald Wooley, and Colonel J.H. Hay's Third Battalion, 86th ousted the Germans from Monte Gorgolesco. Riva Ridge, though shelled often, was being held against many assaults. Monte Mancinello was in the Fifth Army hands.

More counterattacks were expected on Belvedere, which now belonged to the Americans. The tank units attached to the Tenth Mountain Division started upward to hold the mountain. Engineers placed long strips of half-pound dynamite packages on the roads, in the hope that the explosions would destroy the mines. But when a tank took a shortcut, it promptly hit a mine. The tank went up in flames. A few seconds before its 75-mm ammunition exploded, one of the engineers ran up, climbed through the tank turret, and pulled out the commander. Three other tank men were killed.

On another mined road, a bulldozer suddenly flew into the air. The driver was hurled skyward for 30 feet; then, miraculously, he landed without a broken bone.

Monte Belvedere's soft colors and gentle terrain looked sad in the daylight. The relentless artillery fire had melted the snow, and the earth was pockmarked and blackened. Bushes were uprooted. The Italian farmers' beautiful olive trees, though bare in February, had no branches left. The tree trunks were split open as if so many axes had been at work. All the scattered little farmhouses lay in ruins, and the deep, precise trenches dug by the Germans on the Belvedere summit no longer connected with one another. Instead, the holes were filled with rocks and sand and bodies. The dead were strewn all over the area.

Only twenty-four hours had passed from the beginning of the battle for Belvedere. Now the summit was in American hands. But the victorious men of the 85th had little hope for rest. They were allowed only four hours' sleep, then two hours of guard duty. Likewise, the sentries on Riva wondered what the night would bring. Already, the Mountain Troopers had beaten back several German counterattacks. The previous November, other American troops had been driven from Belvedere. Surely the Germans would try to wrest this mountain from the 85th and 87th regiments. In the valley, General Hays minced no words: "Mt. Belvedere and the occupied ground will be held at all costs."

CHAPTER

9

Charge Across the Apennines

Hopes also ran high at the headquarters of German Field Marshall Kesselring. Although dissatisfied with many of his military men, Hitler still considered Kesselring one of his most capable generals—stubborn, ruthless, brilliant. The field marshal's record was as well known as his attitude toward the Allies. "They'll have to buy every yard of Italy with blood," Kesselring liked to say. After holding the north of Italy for more than a year, he bluntly told his troops: "If necessary you must lay down your lives for the Fuehrer! Sell your skins as dearly as possible!"

Kesselring's own skin had been badly injured in a recent accident. On the road between Bologna and Forli, his car collided with a mobile cannon. The driver escaped injuries. When someone later asked the driver how his commander in chief was getting along at the hospital, he said: "The field marshal? Oh, he is doing fine. But the gun had to be thrown away."

Kesselring soon returned from his hospital bed and a short leave. He immediately raced to his headquarters in Recoaro to survey the overall situation. At this point the German commander was only worried about the increasing partisan activity. German Intelligence now estimated that Italy's partisans were two hundred thousand strong. They were being supplied by the Allies from the sky. Every day, Kesselring got word of another sabotage or ambush. Not even the most brutal treatment seemed to stop them. Yet he was confident that he could defeat the advancing Americans. He promised they would never reach the Po. Hitler's propaganda chief picked up the field marshal's promise, and German newspapers were full of assurances that the "larder of Europe will remain German."

Kesselring was well aware of the Tenth Mountain Division. Secret German documents were later found describing the troopers as "physically superior specimens, sports personalities, mountain experts, an elite outfit." But the field marshal also knew the quality of his own troops. His Army Group C was a powerful one. Many of the soldiers had five years of battle experience. They would be able to stave off the inexperienced American troopers with their five *weeks* of combat. Kesselring's Panzer Grenadiers and his 334th Infantry Division contained Bavarians and Austrians. Who knew mountain warfare better than these men from the Alps?

In the meantime, however, the Tenth Mountain Division kept holding Riva Ridge and Monte Belvedere against savage counterattacks. General Hays and his company commanders rotated their troops, so that the Germans always faced battle-fresh Americans.

Apart from hanging onto the hills, Mountain Troopers were getting ready to make brutal attacks against other Kesselring outposts. Shortly after dawn on February 23, several eager battalions of the 85th and 86th headed northwest of Belvedere. As the sun rose, they stormed Monte della Torraccia. The troopers lashed out with bayonets, knives, gun butts. One rifleman was said to lug a bow and arrow next to his traditional weapons. (Tenth Mountaineers still swear that he got several victims with his arrows.) It took only one day to scale Torraccia. The troopers dug in on the summit. During the next twenty-four hours they were hit—but not dislodged—by some one thousand enemy shells.

Meanwhile Monte Gorgolesco, Monte Castello, and Monte della Casellina had fallen to the Americans. Sometimes the troopers moved so swiftly that ammunition, water, and rations ran low. But morale always ran high. Along with their love for the mountains, the troopers felt strongly about each other. Ever since Camp Hale, comradeship was a bond that cemented each company into a fierce fighting unit. Inspections and formalities like saluting were held to a minimum in the field. "It's often difficult to tell the officers from the men," one soldier wrote his mother. "Half the time you might be talking to a general and think he's a yardbird from the ranks."

During a reconnaissance patrol in the snow-covered Apennines in Italy, two members take aim with their rifles while still wearing their skis. *(U.S. Army photograph)*

General Hays had great faith in his troops. After proving themselves in night climbs, they would be just as efficient in the forthcoming daylight action. In early March, the Tenth Mountain Troopers were put to their biggest daylight test. The Germans had to be chased from the remaining high Apennines ground. The first two objectives were 3,308-foot Monte Terminale and equally tall Monte della Vedetta. Enemy mortars and artillery didn't stop the two infantry regiments for long. Both mountains were seized within hours. The 86th next struck for Iola, a hamlet on a hill just beyond Monte Terminale. Here Kesselring's diehards had barricaded themselves in cellars of farm buildings. The Germans kept firing their machine guns through windows; whenever one soldier perished, another would take his place. It was this kind of battle spirit that had earned the Germans their reputation during World War II. Now facing the Tenth were men who would fight from house to house, wall to wall, until they had no ammunition left or everyone lay wounded or dead. While this battle went on at Iola, American tanks ground uphill; from the crests, they sent high explosive shells into other Kesselring positions.

During the next few March days, the Tenth Mountain Division really "found its combat feet," according to one officer. The division managed to advance 5 miles, clearing out one hill after another. The thrust proved to be a cruel one, however, claiming high casualties on both sides. Among the American dead was Technical Sergeant Torger Tokle. Only twenty-five years old, Tokle would always remain famous as one of the world's great ski jumpers. His many friends in the division flushed with anger at hearing the news of his death. During the next few days, the Tenth fought even harder.

The battle of Castel d'Aiano was a particularly deadly struggle. It took place in the bright spring light, and the sun shone down on the Mountaineers moving from bunker to bunker and field to field for three bloody days. Only the fittest survived. Despite the horrors, one field artillery NCO wrote in his diary: "You take one ridge and there's another one just like it staring you in the face. Maybe someday we'll run out of ridges."

But those mountains were precisely what the Tenth had come for. There were so many of them that the General Staff had to assign code numbers, which grew higher every day. Hill 820, 880, 926, 928, 1083—all were snatched from the foe. With each summit won, the Americans would be blasted by artillery from somewhere else. The troops got little rest. Each day took its toll of the wounded, who had long journeys ahead of them: to the battalion aid station, the evacuation hospital, and then to Naples and a ship home.

Medics of the 10th Mountain Division bring an injured skier down from the top of a ridge on the Apennines Mountains in Italy.
(U.S. Army photograph)

Unexpected luck came to the Tenth during one night's engagement. When a unit of the *Jaeger* (Hunter) Division arrived to relieve their comrades, Mountain Troopers got there first and captured an entire battalion headquarters staff. It happened so fast that the Germans didn't know what struck them. The 29th Panzer Grenadier Division was also weakening, and Kesselring had to order reserves to replace casualties. Intelligence reports now told how bleak the German position was. Captain George Earle, in his history of the 87th, noted the following, derived from Intelligence sources:

> The morale seems to have deteriorated. This is partly due to the pounding they had just taken on this front, and partly to the news from other fronts. They were well oriented on the situation at home, and they knew the war was lost. The crossing of the Rhine and the fall of Cologne had been a severe blow.
>
> While the average German is a potential deserter, the measures to prevent desertion have increased and become more brutal, working mercilessly, not only against the family of the deserter, but against his commanders and associates. Any German sergeant has the authority to shoot all suspected deserters.

Some Germans got away with white flags and into American lines before anyone could harm them. American Intelligence officers would immediately talk to the deserters. Why had they done it? What had brought them? Quite often, the former enemy had come into the American fold because of a broadcast. These broadcasts were made through hidden loudspeakers. The message, always in German, could be heard by the other side. The words went something like this:

> Attention! Attention!
> This is a voice from the other side. This is soldier speaking to soldier.

As has often been the case you have been used for a job which is particularly dangerous. You have suffered heavy losses the last few days.

Do you remember the counterattack against Monte della Torraccia where your company was almost destroyed?

They're asking too much of you. You are riflemen fighting against tanks.

It is the ambition of your major to get a decoration.

Major Ruffe, are you listening? Do you really want to get the Knight's Cross? You have already lost one arm in this war, and now you are on your way to losing a battalion.

And so it would go, almost every day, whenever the guns were quiet. It was the work of the Psychological Warfare Branch of the Fifth Army. The results of this "words instead of shells" action got better every day.

Everywhere, Americans sent prisoners to the rear. Even an engineer had six of them in tow. He later explained: "I walked into a farmhouse looking for booby traps when out of the corner of my eye I spotted a fellow in the next room. I swung my carbine around and told him to get out of there. Much to my surprise, five more came out. They were begging me not to shoot them. They'd been told that Americans shot their POWs."

Some twelve hundred prisoners of war were taken in just a few March days. Many of the POWs showed their mettle by marching in cadence, even as artillery banged away. But other Germans just slipped quietly into the prison cages. Their grins showed happiness that it was all over.

A few Tenth Mountaineers also fell into enemy hands. This could happen in the strangest manner. A private of I Company, 87th, was asleep when voices jarred him awake. The tired soldier shouted from his foxhole: "Shut up!" It turned out that he had yelled at some Germans. They took him away, blankets and all. In a house the private promptly fell asleep again. He woke up to see the walls splitting and pulverizing around him. Shortly, his own squad rushed through the dust to free him. A few days later, another GI was taking German prisoners to a cage. Choosing the wrong fork in the road, he marched straight through German territory, where he picked up more POWs and then returned without harm to anyone.

To the Big River!

By mid-March, the situation had changed for the worse for German forces everywhere. The Russians were getting closer to Hitler's Berlin fortress. On the western front, the Allies had reached deep into Germany. Field Marshall Kesselring unexpectedly left to replace Field Marshal Karl von Rundstedt in the West. By that time, the Italian front trembled with Fifth Army successes. The Tenth Mountain Division had now blasted through more than half of the Apennines. The troopers had secured the mountains Grande d'Aiano, della Castellana, Spicchione, della Spe, and the town of Castel d'Aiano. They had ripped much of the important Highway 64 out of enemy hands. The 85th Infantry sat on Pra del Bianco. The 86th controlled Monteforte. The 87th occupied Montecroce and took Monte della Cassellina, also known as Punchboard Hill.

General Hays had reason to be satisfied with his division. In a letter of commendation the general wrote: "You accomplished your assigned mission with magnificent dash and determination. I am proud of you and salute your courage. You have won the confidence and admiration of all troops within the theater!"

Praise showered upon the Tenth Mountain Division from all sides. Field Marshall Harold Alexander, Allied Commander in Chief in Italy, paid his tribute to the troopers. General Mark Clark sent his congratulations, and Lieutenant General L. K. Truscott wrote: "The Tenth Mountain Division has demonstrated on the battlefield its right to be classified as a splendid combat unit, not only capable of undertaking a sustained advance against a well entrenched and wily enemy deployed on rugged terrain but eager to do so. The enemy's estimate of elite mountain troops, after short but bitter experience, is a deserved compliment! . . ."

"Give us a crack at the Po," General Hays pleaded, but the Mountaineers were ordered to stay put. General Truscott would not overextend his lines until he was ready for the great spring offensive.

The lull was welcome. Before the final battles, division members were sent to rest camps. The favorite one was located at Montecatini-Terme, a spa not far from the coast. The troopers relished every moment behind the lines. Hot showers! Good soap! Each man could at last strip off his battle clothes (which were thrown away), step under ornate gold-plated nozzles, and wash off the weeks of grime. Men could shave in peace and put on fresh underwear and clean-smelling uniforms. After sleeping fitfully in dirty dugouts, each trooper appreciated the real beds with sheets and freshly cleaned blankets in the marbled hotels.

At Montecatini, the visitors were treated to hot meals prepared by professional Italian chefs. American doughnut girls stood by with coffee at all hours. Local shops had been fixed up as amusement centers, with games and pinball machines. Italian farmers hawked nuts and almonds. Montecatini offered murals to see, and carriage rides through the streets awaited the battle-tired troopers. In the palatial hotels, it was possible to write a quiet letter or listen to jazz or take in a movie at night. Others preferred sightseeing. Many troopers traveled to Florence, where they strolled in the lush Boboli Gardens or admired the Florentine palaces and villas. In Rome, there were golf tournaments and art galleries and the opera.

Each furlough was like a dream, but at the end of it, there always lurked the foxholes. There would be the dangers of digging in at the wrong spot and of not digging deeply enough. A few sleepless nights would bring back the weariness. And after crawling and scraping along the ground, the dirt would also return. Foxholes held no glamour. War correspondent Ernie Pyle, who knew the infantry and the Tenth, too, perhaps expressed it best: "You're always cold and dirty. You just sort of exist. Standing up or lying down. The velvet is all gone from living."

In addition to the discomforts, there were, of course, the perils of being torn to shreds by bombs, of being hit by shrapnel, by hand grenades, or by rifle slugs that traveled 2,700 feet a second. A man could be stabbed by a bayonet, squashed by an exploding wall, injured by falling bombs. He could be blinded by brick fragments, deafened by antitank guns. A sergeant still remembers how, on a night patrol, "night suddenly turned into day." Someone had tripped a wire that unleashed a flare. Within split seconds, the entire patrol was lit up—perfect targets. When the patrol leader took a forward step, a shoe mine tore off his foot. At about the same time, a sergeant of L Company, 87th, was hit by mortar fire. "It felt like being hit by a sledgehammer," he later recounted. "I lost blood fast."

Bravery was commonplace. A sergeant of the 85th lunged directly at a machine gun that was aimed point-blank at him. Somehow, he overpowered the gunners and then shot them as they fled. Tenth Mountain chaplains would move fearlessly to comfort prone soldiers. An NCO of the 126th Engineers noted in a report: "Every time we'd try to clear the road, the Germans showed their dislike by throwing everything at us. But Lt. McK., Sgt. T. and Pvt. W. were to clear the mines regardless of shelling." The same engineers tried to set up a bridge across the Malandrone River. Three times the bridge was knocked out, and three times the brave workers put it up again. Ambulance drivers of the 87th drove along the same Malandrone River with a cargo of wounded. They knew what to expect. The desperate enemy was again blasting away with mortars around a curve. Many medics were killed. Without fail, other medical corpsmen would try to sneak through.

The final spring offensive was planned for April 12, 1945. The British Eighth Army would push along the Adriatic coast. Beside them would be the American Fifth Army. But once more, the Tenth Mountain Division was chosen to fight in front of all the Allied units, a sort of dagger through the last Apennine chain. North of Vergato, the mountains were steeper than Belvedere, with plenty of rock cliffs. Assault preparation had taken much time. Supply officers had to write their requisitions for more weapons and ammo. Italian mule trains had to shuttle with these supplies. Signalmen received fresh bales of wire and radios; engineers accumulated batches of new mine detectors, shovels, picks. Armored bulldozers had to clear roads for the tanks, and men of the 126th built culverts and graded roads so that vehicles could get through. Special cages for POWs were constructed, and some men attended a new weapons school.

By D day, April 12, officers had studied aerial photos and terrain sketches. Road maps of the Po Plain were issued. The troopers waited tensely for the signal.

But that morning word came through that the offensive was off. The reason was a weather report received at General

Lucian Truscott's Fifth Army headquarters. It read: "Clouds banked up over the south slopes of the mountains and fog is rolling in from the sea." It was too cloudy for aircraft, and the general had decided that the Tenth Mountain Division must have air support. This was going to be one of the biggest attacks of the war in Italy. During the afternoon, the situation did not improve and the attack had to be delayed.

On the 13th, the troops received the news that their President and Commander in Chief, Franklin Delano Roosevelt, had died. It would not be a good day to begin the last, decisive attack. So again the soldiers waited. The delay set many of them on edge. They had no choice but to sweat it out.

The hours ticked by slowly; many cups of coffee were consumed; the receiver remained glued to the general's ear. "Florence blanketed with heavy fog, Pisa visibility one half mile, Grosseto broken clouds of fog rolling in from the west," read the dawn report of April 14. Row after row of fighter bombers, warmed up and armed, sat on all fields, their pilots at the controls waiting for the order.

It was 6:45 and the planes had not yet left the ground. At 7:15 the attack was set back another half hour. At 8:30 the 57th Fighter Group was finally in the air.

General Truscott said: "The show is on."

The last great battle of the Fifth Army in Italy had begun.

Precisely at 8:30, wave after wave of bombers came over the mountains from the south. Men of the Tenth looked up from their jump-off position south of Bologna and got set; they too knew the show was on. Over to their right, on Highway 64, the veteran First Armored was ready. The sky was filled with planes, while the Germans held their breath for the blow.

April 14. 9:00 A.M. The awful nervous tension was released at last. The Italian sky began to show its kindest face. A bright sun highlighted the many blooming fruit trees.

Never had the Italian hillsides seemed lovelier. Then the silence was broken by the sudden, ear-splitting artillery barrage. Before nightfall, some 33,400 shells roared into German positions. At the same time, hundreds of machine guns spewed out bullets.

Fighters whistled into action above. For 40 minutes, Spitfires, Thunderbolts, and Liberators dived and soared over enemy-held towers, strafing, firing rockets, dropping high explosives and oil bombs, then wheeling through 200-foot towers of smoke of their own building. "Give 'em hell," muttered the infantry, as the ground shook.

P-38 bombers plastered Italian ridges just as other P-38s were reducing Germany to a shambles. To the Germans, that April day must have seemed a harbinger of catastrophe. The Russian armies were storming into the Fatherland from the east and showing little mercy. Field Marshal Bernard Montgomery was marching forward through northern Germany. Other Allied units stood only 57 miles from Berlin. Cities already reduced to ruins were still being sacked. The German armies in Italy—almost one million soldiers—would be finished, too. General Hays, Tenth Mountain Division, helped see to that, but it would take nineteen days of uninterrupted fighting.

The task was not an easy one. The Germans had had enough time to prepare themselves in these mountains. And they knew where the final assault would come.

On the first day of the attack, engineers had to dig up some three thousand mines. According to one war correspondent, the German mines were getting varied and plentiful. "There were mines with high trip wires, mines with low trip wires, mines with trip wires at the sides. Glass-topped Topf mines that fooled detecting devices, shoe mines, Teller mines. Some of the mines were rigged to go off even after wires had been cut. Holes six feet deep were packed with dynamite, topped with Topf mines."

In one area, encountered by I Company, 85th, the terrain around every house was mined for a hundred yards, and the houses hid snipers. In addition, German Panzer Grenadiers sat in well-fortified positions. The entire front was now manned by the crack 334th Infantry, and the American air bombardment and artillery didn't appear to decrease their fire strength. Two assault regiments abreast—the 85th Mountain Infantry on the left, the 87th Mountain Infantry on the right —the Tenth Mountain Division pushed ahead.

Colonel David Fowler's 87th shot its way into Torre Iussi in a house-to-house fight. Trouble lurked. The Germans were well protected by sandbags. On some farmlands they sat behind a camouflage of haystacks. Many GIs died before they were able to determine the direction of the shots. Meanwhile, the 85th jumped off near Castel d'Aiano and fought across the Pra del Bianco basin to reach the high ground of the north. It forced its way through a series of hills, the most strongly defended of which was Hill 913. Here the 85th was almost stalled by the enemy's concentrated firepower. The two regiments suffered nearly five hundred casualties on that first day of the offensive.

The next day the attack continued. The 86th had been held in reserve, but now Colonel Clarence M. Tomlinson led his command into battle on the right of the 87th Regiment. The division's swift advance had resulted in a dangerously exposed left flank, so the 85th swung over to meet this threat. As the other two regiments slugged past Monte Pigna and Monte Mantino, the 85th fought a pitched battle in the gap between the Tenth Division and the Brazilians.

At last, the division could move forward, with the British army assisting to the east. On April 16, after Monte Mosca was taken, Mountaineers beat back ten German counter-attacks.

The old ruses could hardly slow the Mountain Troopers now. They were getting used to seeing Italian women and children forced as shields into German trenches. Members of the 87th were not especially astonished by the discovery of a hospital red cross on the roof of a huge ammo dump near Rocca Roffeno. Nor would the old Mountaineers let their guard down when they saw a white flag as a surrender sign. It had often been a trap. A few diehard enemy soldiers would start shooting as soon as the Americans came close. But these desperate tricks succeeded less and less.

In fact, the Fifth Army was forging ahead with precision and coordination. Again and again, American fighter bombers took off from Pisa and lashed out at the few remaining German positions. That mid-April, the Germans had serious trouble: They were unable to cope with the advancing troops. A battalion of the 87th flogged the foe off Montecroce and Monte San Pietro. The aptly-named Monte Sinistro fell, and Monte San Michele was soon in U.S. hands. Tenth Mountain tanks blazed away victoriously at 90th Panzer Division tanks.

Three days had been enough. The German defense fell apart almost everywhere. Tiny postcard villages, already in bad shape, went up in flames. Bodies littered the hot mountains and valleys. Once lovely hillsides were ravaged and the rich olive trees lay in splinters. The blooms had been shot off the apple trees.

But the war was shorter now. The Tenth had broken through. The troopers could finally look into the fertile Po Valley. From now on, the advance could no longer be stemmed.

11

Breakthrough!

Like a mighty avalanche, the Tenth now thundered down from the mountains. The enemy could no longer stop the thrust of these troopers, who carved and ripped a dusty path through the plains. Once-proud Nazi units often waited at the side of the road, wanting to be taken prisoner. Whole German companies gave up without firing a shot. Some of the soldiers were teenage boys, who had been recruited at the last minute and brought to Italy from Germany. These boys were glad to let the Americans surge forward. Only now and then, a hard-bitten Nazi officer would refuse to turn in his arms. Hitler had ordered that he fight until he had no bullets left.

One town after another tumbled: Bologna, Castelfranco, Bomporto, Modena, and still the Tenth Mountain rushed north. The official Army report of the 87th Regiment describes the situation that April:

> The road was a narrow ribbon of Allied territory, stretching mile after mile deeper into German terrain. On either side of the long procession of men and

vehicles, there sat the enemy. Step off the road and you were in German-held land. Occasionally, a stray burp gun would fire to emphasize this. But the enemy mostly hugged their dugouts for the night and surrendered quietly in the morning. Or else, when an American column halted, a German would tap a driver's shoulder, to be searched and waved to the rear. Columns of prisoners, sometimes with partisan guards, strung along the road, headed south. One group of prisoners even caught the festive spirit and cheered with the Italian guards as the American soldiers passed . . .

In the small town of Bastiglia, the Tenth Mountain Division faced stiff resistance. The worst moments occurred from 12:30 to 3 A.M., when confusion competed with exhaustion. Behind the men lay twenty hours of constant marching and fighting over 25 miles. Their great fatigue had been controlled during the day by the excitement of the throngs of happy Italians. But the troopers were now reaching a stage of complete physical exhaustion.

The Germans were still thick inside the town, but badly disorganized. Many times Germans would be upstairs and Americans downstairs, firing at each other through the ceilings. Many soldiers were now in half-stupor states from sheer fatigue. The masses swayed back and forth like the battle lines of ancient Persia. When a German bazooka fired, everyone surged to the rear; then they pushed forward again, firing wildly in all directions.

Prisoners, enemy soldiers, and Italian civilians moved in and out of the dark buildings with the Americans—all in equal confusion. Piles of grotesque bodies, seemingly dead, in the gutters and against the walls were in reality sleeping men. Only the sound of their own firing kept others conscious.

Captain Earle, historian of the 87th, later noted: "Why

there were not more American casualties, even from U.S. bullets, no one will ever know." For sheer volume of fire in a small confined area, Bastiglia was a place of terror. But at last real highways could be used. They were clogged with thousands of refugees traveling from liberated territories. The workers who had been enslaved by the Germans headed home to Naples, Bari, Palermo. The Americans rumbled north on the same highways, which ran straight and level toward the Alps. Private Merrill Pollack noted in his diary with glee: "I'm in the Po Valley now. It's so flat that I'm dizzy." Each truck carried thirty-five to forty troops. The roads trembled under the wheels. As a precaution against Nazi aircraft, the vehicles only rolled at night, without lights.

The drivers could go no faster than 40 miles an hour under these blackout conditions. Sometimes it was so dark that 25 miles an hour was the highest speed. Exhausted men piled on top of tanks. More troopers drove in jeeps. A few lucky officers were able to get hold of staff cars left behind by the Germans, who had lacked fuel for their Mercedes, Opels, Horchs, and other makes. Men of the 86th and 85th rode captured motorcycles, some of which had sidecars. They rode tractors, horses, wagons, donkeys. A whole platoon of the 87th had miraculously equipped itself with bicycles; this was easier than walking.

But a good many of the Tenth Division had to march. They marched 30 to 40 miles a day without complaining. That April week they didn't sleep more than a few hours a night. No one had shaved for days, and the men's bodies were thick with dirt and dust. Troops crossed the "bread basket" of Italy—the region where corn, rice, beans, wheat, and tomatoes were grown. Yet a hot meal was rare. C rations were eaten fast and cold and on the run. There was no stopping now. The men, the trucks, the tanks, and the horses and mules knew only one destination—the Po River.

Early on April 23, the vanguards of two regiments swept through the town of San Benedetto Po, and a few miles farther, they alighted on the Po's south banks.

It was an important moment. The Tenth Mountain Division, of all the Allied forces in Italy, was the first to reach the great waterway. The British, the Canadians, the South Americans, the South Africans, the Jewish brigade from Palestine, and the Poles all crossed the Po later than these American Mountain Troopers.

The men knew that they now steered toward a climax.

The enemy was fleeing. Few commanders had a clear idea of where their own troops or the Americans were. Germans had been ordered to make for the Po and get across by any means. One divisional order captured by the Fifth Army read: "We will cross the river as individuals as best we can. Motorized vehicles will be left behind and destroyed if possible. Horse-drawn vehicles will be taken across if possible, with the horses swimming. Heavy weapons will be discarded, and we will defend ourselves with rifles and machine pistols."

The south bank of the Po was therefore a scene of confusion and a junk pile. German vehicles were run into ditches, overturned, and set afire. Others had been abandoned intact as they ran out of fuel. Still others, including many horse-drawn vehicles, lay in ruins where American fighter bombers and artillery had stopped them.

Speed had been everything, and when the 85th, 86th, and 87th regiments assembled behind the river dikes, their leaders had to solve many problems. To start with, one of the best and toughest officers was out of action. General Duff, "the Terror of Camp Swift," had been wounded when he tried to warn a tank crew about a mine just as it went off. The troopers remembered him well enough as the man who had taught them to endure long marches. It was this Texas training that now helped them. The general was replaced by Colonel William Darby, who had become famous as a Ranger. He had made headlines in North Africa. Shortly, a task force would be named after Colonel Darby.

In the meantime, though, General Hays, the commanding general, knew that he faced more obstacles. That morning, standing near the river with his troops, the general's lean 5' 9" frame was partially hidden behind spring-green willows. At this spot, the Po's width amounted to about 400 yards. The stream ran swiftly. "Well, we got here," General Hays told Colonel Earl Thomson, his chief of staff. "Now let's get across!" It was easier said than done.

General Hays had asked for assault boats, but none had yet arrived. He had asked for fighters and bombers, only to be told that none would be available for the Po crossing. Several air force bases were then being moved, and so couldn't help out with planes.

General Hays had requested aerial photographs which would have shown German positions and artillery installations. But the division had pushed ahead so fast that no pictures had been made. Which would be the best spot to ford the river? What awaited the troops on the other side? It would be impossible to know for the moment.

As the general lifted his field glasses, he felt a pang of impatience. The division had gotten here so fast that no bridging equipment had yet arrived. The Germans, naturally, had destroyed their only bridge. Behind General Hays, the trucks were double-parked, and the signal units, who would furnish communications after a crossing, carried no cable thick enough for the big river.

Nor would there be time to prepare the necessary artillery barrage. Yet the general realized that the Po River—like the Rhine, the Oder, the Elbe—would demand a supreme military effort. Rivers were always big natural barriers. The general's glance shifted across the green waters to the north bank. No trees blocked the way, and visibility was clear. The general turned to another officer. "Did you take a look?"

Both officers were puzzled. They could see German foxholes across the river, but not a single soldier was in evidence. Had they fled? Had the river been abandoned? Would there be no resistance at all?

Unfortunately, because of the absence of Intelligence reports and aerial photos, the general couldn't know that the defenders had dug new and better camouflaged foxholes. They were waiting with their machine guns at the ready. Nor could the Americans know that the enemy had mobile pieces of artillery just behind the new front line on the other shore.

Despite the uncertainty, General Hays was ready to forge ahead. Every minute of waiting would give the enemy forces additional time to prepare a strong stand. Each moment's hesitation would allow the enemy time to regroup.

Yet it took a good part of the morning to get the landing craft from corps headquarters south of Bomporto to San Benedetto Po and then to the water itself. Finally, the 126th Engineers reported that the first fifty assault barges were being unloaded. None of them had a motor or any sort of shield against shells. Each boat weighed about 450 pounds. It was gray-green, with enough room for twelve men and the two engineers responsible for rowing.

At his command post, the division commanding officer turned to a colonel. "At 1200 hours [noon], the 87th Infantry has the honor of crossing the Po," General Hays said solemnly.

12

Crossing the Po River: "And the Tenth Shall be the First"

The general drew bold strokes on a map before him. "These are the bridgeheads," Hays said. According to his plans, the 87th would cross first. It would be protected by the 85th, which had strung out along the south shore. The 1125th Armored Field Artillery, with its big 105s, would lend a hand. The 86th Regiment would be held in reserve for now; it could follow at night.

Some of these troopers were commanded by Colonel J. H. Hay, whose Third Battalion, 86th Infantry, had first cut off Highway 9, north of Bologna, rushed off to Bomporto, and now sat several miles downstream. Colonel Hays had one tank company, a company of engineers, an armored cavalry troop, and an artillery battalion. Just as more ships were being trucked toward the dikes, German artillery, 2,500 feet behind the north shore, burst into action. The first of many big shells ripped across the river. Immediately, American 81-mm mortar and artillery replied. Set up on their bipods, the mortars' answer was loud and long. Farther back, U.S. tanks and more artillery had massed and shells now roared over the heads of the mortarmen. Just in case, General Hays had requested and received twelve British cannons, with their Medium Royal Artillery crews.

11:53 A.M.

Embarkation! Two platoons of forty-eight men, belonging to the First Battalion, 87th Regiment, ran toward their boats. Fresh fire lashed shores and water. This time, the Germans were also pounding away with 88-mm antiaircraft guns. Instead of pointing these cannons into the sky, the enemy's ack-ack bombarded the Po and everything on it that moved.

All the same, the first four boats began to cross the swirling, noisy river. ("It was longer than crossing the Atlantic," one man remembers.) The crews rowed and rowed; barrage or not, the four boats got to the other side. Shakily, the men jumped ashore and immediately dug in.

Others followed bravely, despite the high velocity shelling. As one crew manned the oars, a sergeant kept shouting "one-two-one-two!" for courage and speed. The screaming artillery didn't bother the occupants of one craft. Here the men were heard singing: "From Kiska to the Alps / Where the wind howls through our scalps!"

A colonel of the 87th Headquarters staff astonished everyone. In the middle of the embattled river, the colonel suddenly broke out in the song "The 87th is best by far." His men joined him as machine gun bullets sang another tune over their helmets. Meanwhile, several B Company soldiers turned their boat into a racing shell. Its lieutenant counted cadence as though in a university race and ten experienced men were rowing. The crossing was made in record time.

One after another, the little assault barges kept coming. The current was stronger than anticipated and several oars were lost in the waves, but the men were eventually carried to the other shore anyway. So far, the Germans had scored only a few direct hits. Once a shell exploded under a hull, and men shot skyward. With all the splashing, some boats couldn't help capsizing. For the heavily loaded soldiers, it was difficult to swim.

In the meantime, several boats of the 87th had hit the sandbars that blocked the way to shore a little farther east. As the ships' bows bit into the sand, the men fell forward with a jolt. They got soaked. At still other locations, a few troopers found themselves in deep water. They swam for their lives. Several boats were seen floating aimlessly downstream, with not a soul aboard. At another spot, a private stood in the river to his neck. He had both hands raised, holding up an urgently-needed radio set. Unfortunately, it had already become wet enough to make it useless. Some landing craft were so top-heavy with men and gear that they almost sank. Yet wave after wave of Americans continued moving toward their goal. An eager private first class saw that his assigned craft was full. "Take the next one!" he was told. "No! I'm coming!" he shouted. To everyone's surprise, the boy just hung onto the stern and was towed across the river.

Not all GIs were that courageous. At the height of the German barrage, a young officer suddenly crawled under a tank and cried. His troops shoved off without him. For another boy, already aboard, the blistering machine gun bullets and shrapnel from the 88s were just too much. He jumped into the water. He was killed there while his buddies got through without harm.

On the Po's north shore, wherever the banks were the steepest, the soldiers could see Italian men, women, and children. The civilians stretched out their arms, eager to help the arriving troopers-turned-sailors. A mile behind them, mounted on trucks, hidden in ravines and in the yards of farmhouses, German antiaircraft still fired. Despite it all, the 126th Engineers unloaded their men and then recrossed the stream for twelve more. Some hardy types made twenty trips.

By six o'clock that afternoon, the entire 87th had reached the other side and was already pushing inland. The 85th followed. "We felt very naked," one man wrote of the crossing. A staff officer later noted in his report: "A more detailed study of the river and the enemy situation would have disclosed that antiaircraft artillery would be able to interfere with the crossing troops." It was also later determined that a lower river spot might have had advantages. This bridgehead would have been out of the German gun range. Many times, radio and telephone contact were lost altogether between the two shores.

All through the night, supplies arrived on the south shore —engineering supplies, pontoons, cables, wires, gasoline, food. The jeeps and trucks were now triple-parked. All night, too, more men were ferried to the north shore. Now it was the 86th's turn, and they had moonlight for their river trip. For those units who followed the next day, life would be easier. Already, the 24th Engineer Pontoon Battalion had decided where their bridge had to go. All the necessary measurements were made, and the pontoons were already being assembled. In time, a colonel's jeep would race so eagerly across that the vehicle would reach the other side almost empty. Packs, cameras, ammo spilled into the river. Even the maps fell in the water.

That night troopers pushed toward farmhouses to silence machine gun nests, and then across a smaller river, the Mincio, to drive the Germans from their 88 positions. On their way north, members of the Tenth were suddenly face to face with five hundred enemy soldiers, who just as suddenly gave up. It turned out that these men had been en route to help their comrades along the Po—reinforcements that had come too late.

The skirmishes continued through the next day. The sandy river crossing and the foxhole digging often had unexpected results. Once across the Po, a sergeant set up his machine gun just as two Germans opened fire on him. His gun "clicked and jammed." It was filled with river sand. Another GI came to the sergeant's rescue.

Again and again, the retreating Germans were unprepared for American speed. Plans had called for the Tenth Division to smash the lines and then let other divisions finish the job. But the Tenth's momentum was so great now that the troopers just swung on. A unit of the 87th came upon *Wehrmacht* soldiers sitting peacefully in a restaurant, waiting for dinner to be served. A squad of the 86th would never forget how they settled down for a few hours' rest in some stone houses previously occupied by Germans. A knock roused the Americans and there stood the innocent German quartermaster, bearing a basket of bread and meat. He had no idea that the Americans had come this far. At Villafranca, a Focke-Wulf plane landed as if the airfield still belonged to the Germans. Too late. Shots taught the pilot otherwise.

Meanwhile, L Company, Third Battalion, 87th, marched toward a small town. They could see groups of soldiers walking in the square and standing around talking. Some of them just across the bridge waved amicably to the Americans. Soldiers pedaled by on bicycles, believing themselves miles from the front lines. At first the Americans took them for friendly partisans because of their nonchalance. But in the moonlight the U.S. lead scout recognized the uniform of the Nazis. He yelled to them, ordering them across the bridge with their hands up. The nearest group standing in front of a building took his command with good humor. They laughed and talked among themselves as though it were a joke. Finally one of them shouted in alarm, *"Americani!"*

Nearby, a Colorado-born lieutenant single-handedly stopped a convoy of three hundred men in flight. Their trucks were loaded with important files and papers. The lieutenant directed his catch to a POW camp. To everyone's amazement, a freight train full of troops was still chugging along near Villafranca. No one on the train was aware that the Americans had come this far. The locomotive became a good target. After it exploded, the train came to a hurried stop. Mountain Troopers ran forward to surround the freight cars. Totally puzzled soldiers raised their arms.

Perhaps one of the Tenth's most extraordinary episodes took place near the river. Taken prisoner a few days before, Private John Willis, of the 87th, was made to walk for fourteen hours by the Germans. He managed to escape. After hiding in the bushes, he dashed into a foxhole just as other German units ran off. Men from A Company saw Willis. What was an American uniform doing in *that* foxhole? And why did this American have his hands up in surrender? Was it all a ruse? Had the Germans perhaps dressed one of their own people in a dead American's tunic? Because this had happened before, the men of the 87th were ready to shoot this soldier on the spot. Even the captain who first spied Private Willis suspected a trick.

Someone yelled: "Don't kill him! He's American!"

But the captain didn't trust Willis. An eyewitness later recorded the conversation between the two:

> "What outfit you from?" the officer asked.
>
> "87th," Willis answered.
>
> To the captain, this seemed too pat to be true.
>
> "What company?"
>
> "Headquarters, Third Battalion."
>
> "Who is commanding officer of K Company?"
>
> Willis became tense: After a long, fear-stricken moment, he said: "Captain Eddy, sir."
>
> "How about L Company?"
>
> "Captain Duncan."

"Hand the man a rifle and let's go!" the captain said.

The Po crossing led the Tenth to a mad, headlong movement across the Po Plain. The old Shakespearean town of Mantua fell. Villafranca was occupied. Everywhere, the division was greeted by signs, posters, streamers reading: "VIVA I LIBERATORI!" The liberators did indeed get a warm welcome from the Italian population. Flowers flew toward the dusty jeeps. At whatever hour the Americans showed up, all the inhabitants of a village or town would line the sidewalks in joyous groups. Even at four in the morning, children ran along the sides of vehicles. Women jumped on the trucks' running boards to embrace the flower-covered, grinning Americans. "*Eviva!*" shouted the people.

In one town, the drivers saw a middle-aged man "leaping up and down in a frenzy, with tears streaming down his face." The British, the French, and the Brazilians—in fact, the entire Allied armies in Italy—were received with similar enthusiasm. What our troops had come to call the Promised Land was indeed a land of milk and honey, to say nothing of wheat and rice and fruit and livestock. While southern Italy lived on semistarvation rations, the Po Valley residents now lacked only tobacco, sugar, and a few other luxuries. Earlier, most of the "larder" had been shipped to Germany, but because of the destruction of their oil refineries, and with railroad and highway bridges out, movement to and from Germany had now become a tedious and hazardous process, and they were not able to loot the country as thoroughly as they had done previously.

Thus, despite a long German occupation, the Italians of the Po Plain found fresh food for the grateful Americans. Even at four in the morning, the natives would be there, offering bread, cheese, apples, tomatoes, boiled eggs. The change was delightful for the troopers, who had been living on cold rations. One man wrote home that camps for a night were set up in "wine shops, shoe shops, villas and on hillsides, but they were only momentary, and we would soon be off again." During one night, General Hays ordered the trucks and other vehicles to stop by the side of the road.

"Park your convoys and go to sleep!" he commanded. Although they were in the middle of the enemy, nothing happened that night. "The Lord had us by the hand," General Hays liked to say.

But the war was by no means over. When parts of the Tenth approached Verona, a beautiful medieval city south of the Alps, the troopers' ears suddenly hurt with a terrible explosion. The retreating forces had dynamited all but one bridge across the Adige River. The detonations were so massive that the GIs could feel shock waves in their jeeps. By the time they reached Verona, not a single pane of glass was left in the fine old buildings. Nothing moved in front of the ancient palaces. Italians huddled in churches.

Task Force Darby now sped across Verona's cobblestones. American tanks clanked into the old town squares and along the main streets.

The Germans were gone. They left behind their big posters that had warned the population: "Your district may become a battle area within the next weeks. In order to save your life and property, it is in your interest to evacuate this district. Whoever shall be found in this area after that date shall be shot as a spy without challenge." The warning was signed: "The Commandant of the German Troops."

That April 26, 1945, Verona's narrow streets filled up with citizens celebrating the occupiers' departure. Some even claimed that the war was over for good! Had the Germans indeed surrendered? Surely, they could not hold out much longer. Hitler had lost his best troops and almost all his equipment, and German cities lay in ruins. Only the insane wanted to continue the fight. Yet there was still enough of a German spark left to roughen the lives of the Tenth Mountain Troopers. Several more battles loomed just ahead.

CHAPTER

13

The Hot Pursuit

All the way through the Po Plain, the pursuit went on. "We sure have Jerry on the run," wrote Bill Craine, 605th Artillery, to his parents in Ohio. "The Tenth has us on the go to *keep up* with the enemy! We get into one position to fire a few rounds and then pack up and take off again."

The race was on to the Alps, which could now be seen on clear days, like a narrow, silvery flag.

The war and the killing were not yet over. There were many "last" battles, and the spearheading Tenth never knew where the next shot would come from.

Just northwest of Verona's bastions, the 87th reached a small town named Bussolengo, famous for its wine and its charm. Troubles waited, along with the local population, who welcomed the Americans into town. Lilacs hung on trellises, and boxes full of spring flowers hugged the house walls. Offering their gifts, the people stood on the square. Women had cooked spaghetti, and the hot food was passed into jeeps and among the exhausted soldiers. Girls danced with joy and men shook the Mountaineers' hands. Then, in the middle of all this

118

happiness, a forgotten 88-mm antiaircraft gun, on a rooftop, turned directly toward the crowds. The gun was manned by a German who had stayed behind. The shooting began and the whole town trembled. Women let out screams. Children ran. Civilians were wounded. By the time the Mountaineers silenced the gunner, the joys of liberation lay smashed. War was bitter up to the last moment.

A few miles from Bussolengo, the 87th was pinned down once more. German artillery fire, although it missed, stopped one tank in its tracks. The tank man had become sick with fear. His Sherman rolled forward a few yards, only to stop again. Its guns were inert. A colonel saw it and shouted, "Go!" When the tank still didn't advance, the colonel sprang out from behind a stone wall. He waved his revolver and his officer's cane. Then he pounded on the tank with his stick. "GO!" And it went.

The 85th, moving north from Villafranca to the lakes, was faced by a German suicide attack. The last fanatics of Hitler's army raced forward shooting. It was madness: The Germans were mowed down by machine-gun fire.

Most of the time, however, arms flew up in a gesture of surrender. The POWs were then assembled and marched off, hands folded over their heads. This way, they couldn't conceal any guns. As few as ten troopers might be able to take one hundred or more prisoners. Sometimes two troopers did it. One sergeant who had been with the 87th since Kiska knocked at a large barn northwest of Verona. A German sergeant came out.

"You're surrounded!" the American told him. "Bring out all your men."

Thirty gave up this way, and the trooper earned a decoration. He had been alone.

Sometimes, too, the Mountain Infantry was so intent in their rush to reach the white shimmering mountains that the

artillery had to do the POW-gathering. Other support companies and *partigiani* were mopping up, too. Far behind the
Americans now, the Po River had become a trap for thousands of Germans.

The will to fight had left many of Hitler's warriors. They
were dead tired of war. They had seen too much and heard
too much. They had fought in Russia, France, and Greece,
and they had been beaten everywhere. They worried about
their wives and their sweethearts and about parents at home
who were being destroyed from the air. They worried about
army friends. Had such and such a corporal died in Poland?
Was this officer still a prisoner of the Russians? Did he survive? *Feldpost* (field mail) was no longer delivered. Hundreds of thousands of Germans were cut off from one another.

Whole companies sat down and waited for someone to
capture them. In these last weeks, the Fifth Army took
150,000 prisoners. Passing Mountaineers simply pointed the
way to the rear and hurried on. Some Germans tried to surrender to chaplains, some to war correspondents. Whole battalions gave themselves up. They were disarmed, loaded into
their own trucks, and started back along the road that would
lead them to a stockade. One entire field hospital, complete
with nurses and ambulances, was captured and sent to the
rear under its own power. Some of the German veterans had
actually lost their units. Uniformed men stumbled around
northern Italy in search of their officers. German teenagers,
drafted into the conflict during the last months, lost their rifles. The youngsters often had no idea of where to go or how
to find food. These abandoned soldiers roamed all over the
countryside. It was a better fate to be taken by the Americans
than to fall into the hands of partisans. No one knew for sure
how many Germans were shot by Italians. Altogether, the
Tenth Mountain Division took 11,000 prisoners.

The turning point had come. All the way to blue Lake

Garda, along the excellent highways built by Mussolini, there was the debris of a lost war: burned-out German tanks, smashed trucks, punctured steel helmets, bodies of men. The carcasses of countless horses and donkeys lay rotting.

The U.S. Air Force was still strafing without mercy. The sky was theirs at present and the planes made the most of it. British fighters gave the Germans a taste of what England had endured some five years earlier. The British Eighth Army fought with a special joy beside the U.S. Fifth. While the latter battled westward toward Turin and Milan and the lakes, the English marched eastward toward Venice and Trieste, toward the finish.

The war was now ended for Benito Mussolini, the former Italian dictator. Some Mountain Troopers would soon fight their way to the leader's lakeside villa. Meanwhile, it was no secret that everything had gone wrong for him. After being discharged by the Italian king in July 1943, Mussolini had sold out to the Germans. But he had learned to hate them. His best Blackshirt chiefs shot themselves, or were shot by Hitler's troops, or were assassinated by the *partigiani*. In their revenge to get at the guerrilla fighters, Hitler's SS (*Sturmabteilung,* Storm Troopers) brought terrible suffering on the local people, to Mussolini's grief. He could see how innocent women and children—his Italians—had been shrunk and dwarfed by hunger from the long war years. In the last minute, torture was heaped on torture. Just before his own death, Mussolini confided in his diary: "The agony is atrociously long. I'm like the captain of a ship in a storm; the ship is wrecked and I find myself in the churning ocean on a raft which it is impossible to guide or govern. No one hears my voice any more." Mussolini's voice was stilled on April 28. A partisan leader shot him point-blank.

Organized into brigades of varying sizes, the north Italian partisans still proved to be valuable allies. These patriots kept harassing the enemy, cutting supply lines, raiding towns, stealing equipment, and making life hazardous for individuals or small parties foolhardy enough to venture far from base. In some cities enemy troops dared not wander into certain neighborhoods.

When the entire staff of a certain German division was to assemble at its headquarters for a meeting, the partisans learned the hour and informed Fifth Army agents. An attack was arranged: the air force to bomb and machine-gun the house after all the Germans had arrived, and the partisans, lying in wait, to swoop down the hills and capture German and Italian Blackshirts.

The day Mussolini was shot, the Tenth Mountain Division pushed deeper into the Italian lake country. By now, the Mountaineers had ripped a mighty hole through the German lines. Was the gap still studded with guns? The GIs thought so as they hurried toward their final challenges on Lake Garda.

Lake Garda is surrounded by mountains with a narrow strip for a highway, which curves and zigzags. Frequently, the road disappears into tunnels. The encircling hills are not high; they vary between a few hundred feet and two thousand, but the elevations are full of boulders and buttes. At the northern end of the lake, with the Alps ahead, the mountains are quite steep. It was here that the Germans, strengthened by paratroops and Storm Troops, planned to make a stand.

Already, there had been problems at Lazise and Bardolino, two little lakeside resorts. The Germans fired out of tunnels, using the arches as gunports. Crack German troopers in the town of Garda were awaiting the 87th. According to Intelligence, the enemy had self-propelled guns and artillery—and a plan. The mountaineers were to be delayed so that other fleeing Germans could reach the Brenner Mountain Pass, through which they could get back to Germany. The Tenth was to seal off this escape route.

When the 87th got to Garda, the situation seemed worse. The enemy was not only installed with 88-mm caliber guns, but also with smaller ones. Moreover, these Storm Troopers were Hitler's great pride and the best available. The fight raged all day, and then continued farther north, at Malcesine. Meanwhile the other companies of the Tenth Division made their pursuit over the mountains and along the blackening, stormy lake. From the west shore, about two miles away, the biggest German guns were pounding. Many shells fell into the British artillery batteries that had joined the Tenth. About a mile north of Malcesine, at Navene, the retreating foe dynamited a tunnel. Two bridges were also useless.

This knocked out the highway. Tenth Mountain engineers estimated that it would take two days to clear the tunnel. If one had been blown, several more might go during the next days—all of this was meant to slow down the advancing Allies. The troopers studied the steep mountain. It could be climbed, but it would require special equipment, such as ropes and pitons, which had been left behind in the Apennines.

There was an alternative, though. It occurred to Lieutenant Fritz Benedict, Intelligence, of the 126th Engineers that the demolished road and the rock-choked tunnel could be bypassed by boat. After searching every villa, hotel, and shed, Benedict finally found a 25-foot motorboat. He even located its owner, a civilian, who would pilot the craft along the lake. In this way they could get some knowledge of what other obstacles lay ahead. The lieutenant and his guide took off in short order. They had barely traveled an hour when German shore guns started to bark. The civilian didn't have the heart to go on.

Just then Lieutenant Benedict was greeted by an extraordinary sight. He detected two sailboats taking off from one of the east beaches of Garda. In the brisk wind, the single-masted cutters soon sped past. A British flag waved from one of them and the American lieutenant could recognize the uniforms of the English artillery support units. To everyone's amazement, the British had lashed 20-ton "Long Tom" guns onto the prows of their borrowed civilian sailboats. Before long, the guns began to bellow out of their deep throats. English shells started to scream across the lake, to hit the Germans on the west shore. Each artillery effort made little colored boats heave and bounce in the water.

But the British amphibious artillery was not alone. One battalion of the 86th Mountain Regiment still possessed seven landing barges. These dated back to the crossing of the Po River. The "ducks" came in handy now. Engineers pushed them quickly into Lake Garda. Loaded down with 105-mm howitzer cannons and much heavy gear, the craft stuck close to the shore, their bows pointed north. German guns still blasted away from both sides of the lake. Artillerymen replied from the assault barges and from the American-held lakefronts.

To those who watched from the shore, it was a frightening spectacle. An officer of the Third Battalion, 86th, made a note of what he saw: "German fire from the north burst in angry black puffs of flak over the ducks—shells sent high geysers of lake water into the air—other shells blasted the cliffs above the fleet and falling rocks were added."

When the boats moved farther offshore, artillery fire increased. "The Tenth Mountain's amphibious undertaking could never succeed," wrote Captain David Brower. "Men couldn't live out there on the lake." All the same, a company of the 86th made a landing on the German-held beach. During the rainy night, men of the 86th also took to boats. Each craft could hold about twenty-five troopers. Unluckily, two assault barges capsized in the high waves and most of the troopers went under. But others got through, all the worse for wear. None of them had slept a full shift since crossing the Po, and it was not easy to face German machine guns and shore batteries and mountain snipers in this state of exhaustion. Yet the 86th continued their push along Lake Garda. They were to be slowed down by still another caved-in tunnel.

Here, one of the war's strange stories took place. The German SS had sent a seventeen-year-old recruit ahead to set a demolition charge. They gave him the dynamite sticks, drills, time fuses, and caps. The charge was to go off an hour later.

The young man didn't have the stomach for this last minute tunnel war. He hadn't been trained yet; he was too young. When he tried to beg off, his SS officer told him to go to work or he would be shot.

"*Ich mach es schon*," the boy said at length. "I'll do it." The young German straddled his military motorcycle and made it to the tunnel, far ahead of the Americans, and long before the Storm Troopers, who were crawling up behind him with a hand-pushed 22-mm antiaircraft gun. It had to go north, and there was no fuel to pull it.

The Germans reached the tunnel about 5 P.M. The SS officer was quite certain that his new recruit had obeyed. Everything must be in order, the holes drilled, the boy waiting to light the fuse after they had passed through. But in his fear and confusion, the young SS man had made a mistake in his timing. The explosion went off at precisely the time when the Storm Troopers arrived inside the tunnel. The detonation rocked everything inside the hollowed walls. Immediately, the German 22-mm ammunition exploded. Bodies littered the ground outside and inside. At least forty Germans died that second. Americans later called it the "Tunnel of the Dead." The boy escaped.

Not long afterward, the enemy artillery got their revenge. This time, men of the 86th happened to be inside another Lake Garda tunnel. They were caught by one deafening shell that killed seven and wounded forty-seven.

Meanwhile, the 87th ran into other troubles, as the regiment advanced along the water's edge. From the surrounding summits, the German *Gebirgstruppen* (mountain troops) were sniping without pause. The 87th sent a few squads after the riflemen. But they had fled over the hills. Then, after capturing some German diesel trucks, the Americans found the mountain roads so narrow and studded with so many switchbacks that it was almost impossible to drive.

In the little village of Spiazzi, violent German fire met the Americans. The troopers counterattacked furiously from the high ground east of the town. The Second and Third platoons and the company command group cut them down, but the remnants kept driving on and got close enough to hurl grenades. Large shells were shot into the buildings, wounding two men from D Company. The riflemen learned to stand back four or five feet from the windows to fire.

One platoon fired into dugouts with rifles, and took prisoners who were confused by the attack from the rear. The platoon soon flushed out an Italian Fascist and threw him in with the prisoners, despite his violent protests. Another German was knocked off his bike by rifle fire, and he and two others in a ditch beside him ran into a building. A bazooka shell in the doorway produced a white flag, and five Germans surrendered. This ended the resistance.

During the stormy, dark night, the company encircled the town in a complicated maneuver. Captain Earle, in his official history, later considered the action at Spiazzi "an outstanding example of a night approach, and a surprise attack from two directions against a fanatical enemy." The garrison at Spiazzi was an NCO school, consisting of about two hundred men. The defenders counterattacked repeatedly and viciously to throw out the attacking Americans. An estimated seventy Germans were killed; about forty were captured. The remainder escaped down the steep bluffs.

The 85th Regiment had its own moments of struggle and glory. During the night of the 29th, Colonel William Darby, of Task Force Darby fame, led a group of men in an amphibious assault across the entire lake. This had not been done before. The "ducks" headed directly for a town named Gargnano. Here the troopers made a landing on Mussolini's lakeside property. The former dictator's castle retreat consisted of thirty-seven rooms. Colonel Darby and his raiders found many important documents. The building was crammed with statues, paintings, and relics. Mussolini himself was already dead. His body hung in the main square in Milan.

Unfortunately, a few enemy troops had made up their minds to die for Hitler even when all was lost. The SS troops

Members march north, near Malcesine, on Lake Garda, without meeting any resistance. *(U.S. Army photograph)*

stood their ground at Nago. They fired with artillery from the top of a hospital. The Mountain Infantry had to seek shelter again, behind cemetery walls, in houses and churches, or flattened to the ground. "I got so used to fear that I no longer felt it," one veteran has said. He was badly wounded at Nago when a German plane dropped its last bomb.

The situation was no better at the town of Riva at the north end of Lake Garda, where the defenders deployed several tanks. At the lakeside resort of Torbole, there was another last-minute tragedy. With peace already near, a member of the German Secret Police beat an imprisoned partisan until he finally broke down and put together a long list of his friends. The SD (*Sicherheitsdienst,* Security Service or Secret Police) man immediately took his list from house to house. When someone opened the door, the SD officer would ask: "Is your name Mario Manzoni?" If the man nodded, the SD would cut him down with a submachine gun. In this savage manner, one hundred partisans died in Torbole. Kesselring's old orders were still being followed, although the field marshal himself was now commanding the last-ditch defense of southern Germany.

Torbole, Italy, meant more last instant tragedy for the Allies. Colonel Darby, who led the Task Force, was conferring with his staff under the lakeside arches. A shell came screaming down, killing Darby and several of his officers.

But Lake Garda was free.

The division had done its job. Nineteen harrowing, uninterrupted days came to an end. Those nineteen days were costly. The Fifth Army lost about 6,400 men in less than three weeks. Among them, 5,000 were wounded and 1,400 were dead.

May 2, 1945. Peace. In Torbole that day one Mountaineer eased himself to the ground and told an officer, "Thank God. I made it."

14

Peace at Last!

The war in Italy was at last over. *Wehrmacht* Group C surrendered. General George Hays, Tenth Mountain Division, delivered the German emissary to Fifth Army headquarters. That same day, Berlin, the German capital, also fell to the Allies.

In northern Italy, a great madness broke loose. Church bells rang everywhere. *Pace!* Peace! Citizens danced in the streets. They hugged the soldiers and the soldiers kissed the local girls. GIs fired their guns into the air.

Some people were just quiet. An officer observed one Mountain Trooper who, still geared for the next phase the next morning, just couldn't believe it all. "He was too stunned," the officer wrote. "He knew he ought to feel more elated than he did."

General Hays knew the price his troopers had paid. It was high. Of the 14,300 who had started out in January 1945, 990 now lay dead. Some three thousand men were wounded. General Hays admitted that his regiments "had been pushed to the limit and done the impossible." They had made the enemy lose balance, never to reorganize again. In a talk to his men, the general spoke of the "spectacular things you troops have done." He predicted that "when you go home, no one will believe you."

General Mark Clark sent congratulations to the division: "You've broken the German army in two!" In a letter to General Hays, General Clark was full of praise:

> Our great offensive which ended in the unconditional surrender of the German forces was spearheaded by the Tenth Mountain Division under your brilliant leadership. Will you please convey to all your officers and men the fact that I look upon the action of the Tenth Mountain Division as one of the most vital and brilliant in the war.
>
> From the Apennines you drove northward with the Fifth Army until the Germans laid down their arms.
>
> You plunged ahead, exploiting the severing of Route 9, and to you came the well-deserved honor of being first across the Po. Nothing, it seemed, could stop your drive, and you went forward to Villafranca, to Verona, up and across Lake Garda . . . Pass to meet the Seventh Army. This is the aggressive spirit of which victory is made. It was a privilege to have you in this command.

U.S. Major General Willis D. Crittenberger, who commanded the IV Corps, wrote: "The splendid performance . . . of the Tenth Mountain Division . . . was such as to evoke great admiration in all military circles." Field Marshal Sir Harold Alexander, Allied Commander in Chief in Italy, eventually told the Mountain Troopers: "Sending your division to Italy was one of the best turns General Marshall ever did me." The troopers clapped their hands when Sir Harold finished his speech. Such applause was not according to army rules.

Maj. Gen. George P. Hays addressing the men of his division. He is congratulating them on the fine work they have performed.
(U.S. Army photograph)

The division got its due from Washington, too. The Mountain Troopers received 279 Silver Stars and 2,810 Bronze Stars. Their commanding officer was also decorated.

After the German surrender in Italy, some of the troopers were finally able to live like human beings again. The Third Battalion of the 86th settled down in a castle on Lake Garda. The men were waited on by servants. A chef prepared the best dishes. There were beds and sheets. The troopers had cars to visit the picturesque villages along the lake. Every day, a small convoy left for Venice, where the GIs turned tourists. They rode gondolas through the canals. They fed the pigeons in the magnificent square. They saw how Venetians made glass. They ate and drank well. Artillerymen played volleyball; in the Alps, classes were taught in advanced climbing. At last, the men had time for their private affairs. A soldier of I Company, 86th Regiment, briefly returned to Male, the little village where he had been born. When he came to his old home, his sister didn't recognize him because he had been thirteen years old when he left. His mother was visiting in the next house. After she was informed about the visitor, she rushed up, "crying and laughing and saying over and over: 'Now I can die happy.' "

Everywhere, men were born all over again. As the Third Battalion, 87th, drove north from the lake country into the Alps, fanning out to the towns of Trento, Bolzano, and Merano, the troopers could finally use their eyes to see beauty once more. An officer of the 87th noted in his diary:

> After the memory of the recent dust of battle, the May colors in the foothills of the Alps seemed unbelievably fresh and vivid. The towns were pastel colored, and more picturesque in architecture than the Italy of farther south. Every view seemed like a children's book illustration.

Elsewhere, soldiers swam in lakes, irrigation ditches, and pools. They relaxed in rest camps. A private named Chris Doscher managed to get a furlough. He found a pilot in Udine, up north, who was flying a hospital plane to Rome. The craft was so old that "the wings practically flapped." But in the Italian capital the private had a glorious time. Doscher rented an apartment and "had a bath every two hours." Good fortune also befell K Company, 87th Regiment. They moved to Solda, a large ski resort, high in the Italian Dolomites. The sun mingled with snow. Skiing was excellent. The troopers also didn't mind the sudden luxury, such as maid service, antique furniture, soap, showers, and well-cooked hot food. Thanks to the discovery of nearby warehouses, K company drank champagne three times a day. Over the bar, a sign read: CHAMPAGNE FREE! BEER 20 CENTS. ONLY YOU WEALTHY GUYS DRINK BEER! It was a strange, new life that wouldn't last long.

Another company of the 87th also received its reward for the long weeks in foxholes. The men were put up in a deluxe hotel in Merano, a famous resort town. Fifteen minutes from there, the Germans had stored the loot taken from many countries. There was a great cache of paintings and other art treasures from Florence. There were bales of silk stockings, warehouses of liquor, five thousand commercial radios, one thousand tons of food, and millions in Italian currency.

Despite these pleasures, duties lay ahead. Some units had to rush north and seal off the Austrian and Swiss borders. The 126th Engineers had to repair the broken-down highways, rebuild tunnels, and reconstruct bridges. Guard duty, prisoner exchanges, and lectures occupied the men. Tenth Mountain officers saw to it that the partisans gave up some two hundred thousand rifles, machine guns, pistols, and other weapons. Revenge had to be curbed and law and order maintained. This was difficult because the Americans often didn't know who was who. Many of the Secret Police now wore civilian clothes. Millions of refugees and freed slaves were on the road. Some of Mussolini's former henchmen showed up in German uniforms. At least one German unit still hadn't heard that Hitler was dead and that the war was over. Colonel Robert Works, 87th, reported to his headquarters: "From Trento to our present location, we ran the gauntlet of thousands of armed Krauts who, in their oafish way, insisted on maintaining roadblocks, manning 88-mm scout cars and mountain guns, and stopping and checking our convoy. No harm was done, but they tested tempers."

Captain David Brower, 86th, ran into similar problems as his Third Battalion rolled toward Bolzano one evening. At a roadblock, German officers claimed that night quarters had been prepared for the troopers. But the battalion didn't take the bait that was dangled as a delaying maneuver. That night, as the 86th drove forward under the command of Lieutenant Colonel Hay, another obstacle loomed. Near Merano a German commander said: "The surrender doesn't apply to us!" According to witnesses, the Germans already "had their hands on the lanyards of their artillery." The Americans put on the lights of all their vehicles, something never done during combat. The message was clear: Peace! The Germans let the battalion through without further ado.

Many days later, on May 16, 1945, the Tenth Mountain Division faced another crisis. Marshal Tito of Yugoslavia was threatening Trieste and some surrounding territory that his nation had always coveted. Tito was set to march across the borders to Klagenfurt, in southern Austria. Although peace had been signed everywhere by now, Yugoslav troops were still armed to the teeth. Both the Americans and Tito's Communists exercised and paraded across the borders from one another. For the next two months, Communist troops were too close for comfort and both sides were slightly nervous.

Tito's men tried to impress the people with a show of strength. Soldiers and pictures were everywhere, and the Italian town names were changed to Slavic, the Italian language dropped. At the same time, the Allies were trying to impress Tito with a show of strength, with planes overhead and tanks on the road. Eventually the friction ended.

During the last week in June, the Tenth Mountain Division organized the first international ski race after World War II. Tenth Division champions, British skiers, and other Allied athletes raced on the snowfields adjoining the 12,461-foot Gross Glockner, the highest peak in Austria.

That summer the snow was superb on the Glockner glacier and the Mountaineers beamed with happiness when one of their own—Sergeant Steve Knowlton, 86th—won the downhill race. For many troopers, this ski meet was a high point of their three months in Italy. Skiing meant peace. The racers were well aware of their great fortune: They were still in one piece. They had not been wounded.

Some of the wounded troopers had to be sent from hospital to hospital. It could take as long as two and three years until a man was well again and it could mean much suffering. Division casualties who had returned to the States found their fellow Americans full of consideration. One man wrote to his buddies in Italy: "The purple heart and a crutch is a hard combination to beat. Taxi drivers are kind, doormen practically carry you into hotels, policemen not only hold up traffic but whistle down cabs for you."

During July 1945, the Tenth Mountain Division boarded troopships in Leghorn and Naples. In all, six transports were required to get the troopers out to sea. Again, rumors were rife. The war in Europe had come to an end, but the war in the Pacific continued. Japan was still refusing to make peace. The Tenth Mountain veterans speculated that they would get orders to the Pacific. This was true. They were slated for the war in Asia.

On August 6, while troopers were still sailing the Mediterranean, important news burst over the radio. An atomic bomb had been dropped on Japan. Everyone aboard the troopship hoped that the historic event also meant the end of World War II.

But Japan held out until August 14. Several units of the Tenth Mountain Division were already in the States by then.

The division was deactivated on December 1, 1945. It was time for the soldiers to go home.

CHAPTER
15

The Mountain Soldiers Come Home

It is said that when a man gets to know and love the mountains the two often become inseparable. The hiker, the climber, and the skier are drawn again and again to the heights. This is also true with the former soldiers of the Tenth Mountain Division. The chance of scaling windswept peaks had attracted many of the men in the first place, and the mountains, with all their dangers and challenges, had left a mark on those troopers who had grown up in the flatlands. Midwesterners would never forget their first look at the white massiveness of Mount Rainier. Southerners would never erase the impact of the Rockies cutting a wide swath across the sky as the train approached Denver; or the huge upthrusts surrounding Camp Hale near Leadville, Colorado. The travelers would always remember the Apennines rolling toward the horizon, and then farther north, the Alps that rose suddenly, crested tier upon tier, aglitter in the sun as far as the eye could see.

By the end of 1945, the members of the Tenth were scattered. They had returned to or settled in the Rockies, to New

England's White Mountains and Green Mountains, the High Sierras, the Canadian Rockies, the Laurentians, even the Swiss Alps. Colorado had left its own impression. Some troopers went back to search for a remote valley, where they could work and raise their families and continue to take daily walks on foot or on skis. Some veterans became civilian instructors at Camp Carson, later named Fort Carson, near Colorado Springs. The Army Mountain and Winter Warfare School was here, which continued to shape military skiers through the late forties. It then switched to rock climbing for elite troops, such as the Special Forces and Marines. (Even now, Fort Carson coaches a handful of NCOs in advanced mountaineering techniques.)

The fighting in Italy couldn't dim the bright attraction some men felt for the West. A few minutes after landing in New York, a lieutenant of the 126th Engineers decided that he would not return to his native Wisconsin. He pulled out a scrap of paper with a phone number he had kept with him since the Camp Hale days, all the way through the Italian hills, across the Po, and even on the little motorboat in Lake Garda. The phone number was that of a rancher in Aspen, Colorado. Lieutenant Fritz Benedict called him from New York. "Remember me?" the lieutenant said across the 2,000-mile distance. "Tenth Mountain Division. You once showed me some acreage. Still want to sell that land?" The rancher said at length, "Maybe. If you come here."

Benedict, who is now a prominent architect and village planner, traveled to Aspen. The rancher kept his promise.

Aspen drew other ex-troopers who had skied there on weekends while at Hale. These men transformed the sleepy mining town into a ski resort by planning ski runs and ski lifts and raising the money. All over America, in Vermont, Michigan, Colorado, and scores of other spots, the ex-troopers got involved; in fact, the demobilized Tenth Mountain Division became the great spark plug for the U.S. ski industry. Many of the biggest ski areas—Sugarbush Valley, Vermont, Crystal Mountain, Washington, and Vail, Colorado, for instance, were established by ex-Mountain Troopers.

All through the late forties and the fifties, the men of the Tenth furnished skiing instruction to the general public. They became ski coaches in schools and universities, and they supervised U.S. Olympic athletes. Bill Bowerman, famous Olympic track coach and jogging enthusiast, served in the Tenth. Many notable ski officials came from the ranks of the division, and men of the Tenth still fill most of the country's ski area management jobs.

Among the hundreds of success stories, there is Peter Seibert's, who helped create one of the larger Colorado ski resorts. In March 1945 he was fighting on Monte Terminale, between Bologna and Florence. The Germans opened fire and Sergeant Seibert was hit in the leg. He put on his own bandage and continued advancing. Two days later, as the 86th Mountain Infantry crawled uphill, a mortar blast seared the soldier's face, smashed his teeth, and shredded his knee. "You will never ski again," army doctors warned Seibert. But all through the sixteen months in hospitals, the Bronze Star winner decided that the doctors must be wrong. A few years after the war, Seibert skied again. Indeed, by 1950, Seibert had become an instructor and a world championship racer.

It was a painful and difficult process. Just as the Tenth Mountain Division made the impossible possible in Italy, so Seibert found the "impossible" financial backing for his Colorado resort, and later for a Utah ski area. During the sixties Seibert and his friends roamed the mountains around Leadville on their cross-country skies, wending their way up and down the vast white mountains. Over there the winter vehicles got stuck! Here, at this point, the food ran out during the "D" Series. Way down below, in its circle of 14,000-foot peaks, Seibert could still see the expanse where "Camp Hell" had been.

The fate of Camp Hale is a story in itself. In April 1945 the U.S. Army decided that it would need a large hospital in Colorado. Building materials were scarce, and an officer decided that much of Camp Hale could be dismantled and then rebuilt elsewhere. Thus, in true military fashion, thirty-five hundred prisoners of war got orders to take the camp apart board by board, plank by plank. Although many of these materials were lost, a large hospital was soon erected at nearby Camp Carson. Then the war in the Pacific ended, and the expected stretcher cases did not materialize. By then, only a flagpole, a few mule barns, a field house, and a service club were left at Camp Hale. For some months, nothing happened to these locked-up structures, and one ex-trooper took his

Former members of the 10th Mountain Division dedicate a memorial to their 990 fallen comrades of World War II near Camp Hale. *(U.S. Army photograph)*

wife to the meadow and lived there in a tent for a time. Honeymooners sought out the nearby forests to fish in the clear streams for trout and to explore the trails. Veterans returned to Camp Hale from big cities like Los Angeles and Chicago and New York.

Suddenly in 1947, the generals remembered how Camp Hale had served the Tenth, and younger men arrived from Camp Carson to try on the snows for size. Like the old troopers, these infantrymen pitted themselves against the winter cold. When the Korean War broke out in 1950, Camp Hale served the Rangers as a special training ground. A few years later, army helicopters got their battle tests here. By then, ski troopers no longer seemed as necessary as during World War II days, and most of the military skiing moved out of Colorado and north to Alaska. There, at various locations, winter travel on skis and winter suvival are still being taught to a select group of infantrymen. Like the Tenth Mountain Division, the men are still garbed in white.

Camp Hale saw some more military action on July 1,

**10th members gather at top of Colorado ski run
on dedication day.** *(A.J. McKenna)*

The 10th Mountain Division reunion in the Colorado mountains.
(Archives of the 10th Mountain Division Association)

Sons of the Division look at list of the fallen.
(Archives of the 10th Mountain Division Association)

1965. That day, the buglers sounded a last retreat. A farewell of thirty volleys echoed across the valley. The flag was lowered. Afterward, the U.S. Forest Service once more took control of the area. If you ever travel there, you will see some ancient barrack walls and flagpoles. You'll also notice an attractive campground.

During the late 1970s the U.S. Army and the Forest Service invested money and time to build the Camp Hale picnic areas, fire pits, hiking paths, a wheelchair trail, and parking spaces at the one-time training camp. In 1980, many former troopers came up for the dedication of the 20-acre "Camp Hale Memorial Campground." It is one of the highest such sites in the U.S.

An army general helicoptered into the mountains from Fort Carson, Colorado. A number of Tenth Mountain Association people were on hand. Max Raabe, the dentist, came with his teenage son. Mac McKenna, now in advertising, brought a daughter. Earl Clark, one of the Association officials, was accompanied by his family.

Not far away from Camp Hale on Tennessee Pass, a 14-ton slab of granite reaches 29 feet into the sky. The stone's Roll of Honor lists the 990 comrades who gave their lives for the division. Each year on Memorial Day, hundreds of ex-troopers assemble at Tennessee Pass to remember their companions. Later, they get together to talk about the old days, to swap tales, or to present their sons and daughters to one another.

16

The Troopers Today

Get-togethers are popular with the division. One typical cele-
bration was attended by more than one thousand persons who
flooded to Vail, Colorado. There, a ski run bears the name of
"Riva Ridge," a name the 86th Mountain Infantry Regiment
would long remember. Almost all the veterans' cars displayed
the divisional emblem, two crossed bayonets topped by the
word "Mountain." During the day, fathers and their teenage
offspring hiked through the nearby ranges, and at night, they
ate and drank and sang: "After twenty years / To the brave
men and the true/We'll honor those who gave the most/To
the old red, white and blue."

On another occasion, the fourteen Association chapters
gathered at Lake Placid, N.Y., site of the 1980 Winter Olym-
pics. Among the one thousand participants were a retired
German *Gebirgstruppen* (Mountain Troops) general and a
colonel who fought the Americans at Monte Belvedere. "Past
differences are long forgotten," said one of the German
officers. "The former adversaries now have a lot in common.
They've been brought together by their love of the moun-

tains. And, of course, the Germans and the Americans are allied through NATO in Europe."

Despite their war experiences, not many of these civilians had touched another rifle or revolver. If you looked at the middle-aged faces, you would have been struck by their tanned healthy looks. Even twenty years after World War II these men looked well because they spend so much time outdoors. Most of the troopers still ski. Some of them who live at ski areas set out every winter morning, in every kind of weather. Other men do hard rock climbs. Tennis tournaments, swimming, and hiking keep them fit.

The fondness for sports also plays a big part in the Tenth Mountain Association. Although its 6,000 members are now located in various parts of the country, they often meet for ski outings and fun races. The families come along, too. Few veterans' organizations are this closely knit, with so many ties and personal friendships. "We have something that keeps us together," the ex-troopers often say. If you ask, "What is it?" the answer will be a familiar one, "The mountains!"

Many of the members settled in high regions, especially in the Rockies, the Pacific Northwest and New England. But there are also Association chapters in the Midwest, California, New York and Washington, D.C. Thanks to the ex-troopers, there is a ski museum at Sugar Hill, New Hampshire and in Vail, Colorado. Tenth Mountain memorial plaques hang on Mount Rainier, Washington and at other locations around the world.

The association of these former mountain soldiers, through a special foundation, has done much civic good, too. The foundation provides yearly scholarships for children and grandchildren of former Tenth Mountaineers. The same organization supports regular ski trips for underprivileged youngsters ages nine through high school. The young people receive all their ski clothes, rental skis, transportation, and

Riva Ridge at the Colorado ski area is named after the battlefield. *(Barry Stott)*

A reunion in the Rockies.
(Archives of the 10th Mountain Division Association)

ski lessons. In summer, the lucky youngsters go camping. Dr. Max Raabe, who created the program some twenty years ago, did it because he wanted to share the joys of wilderness excursions into the high country. Many ex-troopers in other parts of North America have also volunteered as speakers in schools; students are always eager to hear firsthand about World War II history.

There are other good deeds. Some years ago, a flood ravaged Florence, Italy. It was a town the men knew well. The Tenth Mountain Foundation raised funds for the city.

Every few summers, a large group makes a pilgrimage to

An Italian man points out the battlefield at a reunion in Italy.
(Curtis Casewit)

the Italian battlefields. Many of the men take their teenagers along to see where they fought. The little red-roofed hill towns always welcome the former soldiers. The mayors make speeches. Schools close and the Italian children sing in choruses. Work stops for the adults. Banners grace the new houses in hamlets like Vergato, Montepastore, in Rocca Roffeno and Vidiciatico. Onetime Italian partisans lead the way uphill through the fields of Monte Belvedere, and the Ameri-

Italian children at a reunion. *(Curtis Casewit)*

cans follow through the chest-high grasses, past the wild strawberries and the red poppies. Now and then, someone still discovers an old steel helmet under a hazelnut bush or in an ancient trench.

General Hays came back several times to these hills to explain where and why he directed a military movement here. Former high officials, NCOs, and others also visit the American Military Cemetery at Castelfiorentino; the dark, stately cypresses add dignity to the crosses. Every year, an old father still arrives to put flowers on the grave of his son. Italian partisan officers are always on hand when the Tenth returns. Although civilians now, the *partigiani* are eager to see old friends. An older man in Castel d'Aiano remembers the soldiers well. During a recent visit, he told them, "Oh, how can I forget you? You were so young, tall and hearty!"

The war scars are long gone from the roads and tunnels and towns around Lake Garda. But the people still have a warm affection for the liberating Tenth. Tears and words flow often.

The Italians have long forgiven their German occupiers. Only the late Field Marshal Kesselring arouses strong emotions. Because he resorted to the torture and killing of civilians, an Allied court sentenced Kesselring to death. The sentence was later commuted, and the brutal old Nazi commander died a natural death. But in the Piedmont mountain town of Cuneo, there still hangs a marble tablet that promises Kesselring his own future "monument." The tablet reads:

Not of the scorched rocks of the defenseless villages you outraged and destroyed. Not of the earth—where our young brothers lie in peace. Not with the snows of the mountains where for two winters they challenged you. Not with the spring of these valleys that watched you flee. *But only with silence which is harder than any boulder. . . .*

A little farther south, in the port of Genoa, a large statue of a dying soldier mourns the battles that took place and the blood that poured from so many wounds in Europe. "May the people learn their lesson," the legend reads. "May there never be another war!"

The survivors of the Tenth Mountain Division nod in agreement.

Bibliography

The Blizzard. Quarterly. Published by the National Association of the 10th Mountain Division, Ayer, Massachusetts.

Churchill, Winston. *The Second World War for Young Readers.* New York: Life/Golden Press, 1960.

Coquoz, Rene. *The Invisible Men on Skis.* Boulder, Colorado: Johnson Publishing, 1970.

Hauptman, C. M. *Combat History of the Tenth Mountain Division 1944-45.* Fort Benning, Georgia: Infantry School Library, 1977.

McKenna, Mac. *The Return of the 10th to Europe.* New York: Century Records (record), 1969.

Sutton, Felix. *The Illustrated Book About Europe.* New York: Grosset & Dunlap, 1970.

White, Anne Terry. *All About Mountains & Mountaineering.* New York: Random House, 1962.

Index

155

ABOUT THE AUTHOR

Denver-based Curtis Casewit, a member of the U.S. Ski Writers and of the Society of American Travel Writers, is the author of *The Mountain World, The Complete Book of Mountain Sports, The Skiers Handbook, Freelance Writing: Advice From the Pros,* and many other books. He served in Europe with the British Army during World War II. He became so fascinated with the story of the U.S. Mountain Troops who also fought in Italy that he returned to the Italian battlefields after the war. He attended reunions of both the U.S. troopers and the German soldiers who opposed them during the war. The result: the Messner book about these gallant mountain and ski troopers.